Anorexia and Bulimia in the Family

Anorexia and Bulimia in the Family

One Parent's Practical Guide to Recovery

Gráinne Smith

John Wiley & Sons, Ltd

Other Wiley Editorial Offices

John Wiley & Sons Inc., 111 River Street, Hoboken, NJ 07030, USA

Jossey-Bass, 989 Market Street, San Francisco, CA 94103-1741, USA

Wiley-VCH Verlag GmbH, Boschstr. 12, D-69469 Weinheim, Germany

John Wiley & Sons Australia Ltd, 33 Park Road, Milton, Queensland 4064, Australia

John Wiley & Sons (Asia) Pte Ltd, 2 Clementi Loop #02-01, Jin Xing Distripark, Singapore
129809

John Wiley & Sons Canada Ltd, 22 Worcester Road, Etobicoke, Ontario, Canada M9W 1L1

Wiley also publishes its books in a variety of electronic formats. Some content that appears in
print may not be available in electronic books.

Library of Congress Cataloging-in-Publication Data
Smith, Gráinne.
    Anorexia and bulimia in the family : one parent's practical guide to recovery / by
    Gráinne Smith.
        p. cm.
    Includes bibliographical references and index.
    ISBN 0-470-86161-4 (paper)
    1. Anorexia nervosa – Popular works.   2. Bulimia – Popular works.
    3. Caregivers – Popular works.   I. Title.
    RC552.A5S63 2004
    616.85′26–dc22   2003014729

British Library Cataloguing in Publication Data
A catalogue record for this book is available from the British Library

ISBN 0-470-86161-4

Illustrations by Lucy Aykroyd

Project management by Originator, Gt Yarmouth, Norfolk (typeset in 10/12pt Imprint)
Printed and bound in Great Britain by Biddles Ltd, King's Lynn, Norfolk
This book is printed on acid-free paper responsibly manufactured from sustainable forestry in
which at least two trees are planted for each one used for paper production.

To my daughter Jay with love

The mother's place now seems to be, not in the kitchen or the home, but in the wrong ...

Unknown

Contents

About the author

Gráinne Smith has worked for several years on the Eating Disorder Association helpline as a volunteer, putting to good use her training and experience as a former Samaritan. During that time she has spoken to hundreds of carers and sufferers as well as to many professionals.

A founder member, now chairperson, of NEEDS Scotland (North East Eating Disorder Support) and a member of the Mental Health group that developed the Scottish Executive Health Department framework document for eating disorders services in Scotland, she has also taken part in Mental Health and Wellbeing Support Group visits to health boards and presented a petition on eating disorders to the Scottish Executive. She currently works to raise awareness of how poor mental health affects whole families while good mental health underpins physical well-being.

During a long career in primary education, including nine years as head teacher of Fyvie Nursery and Primary School, Aberdeenshire, she enjoyed working with whole families and children aged from 3 to 12. As a writer, Gráinne has had short stories and poems published in magazines and anthologies; while working with Grampian Region she helped write and present courses for teachers and head teachers; she has also written many educational materials including co-ordinating and contributing to the pack "Fyvie Castle – Its Life and Legends".

Foreword

I am delighted to be asked to write the foreword to this book by Gráinne Smith. I think it is a unique contribution, as it gives voice to a neglected group in the management of people with eating disorders (i.e., carers or family members). Gráinne not only speaks from her own personal experience, she has also been involved in running one of the telephone helplines for the Eating Disorders Association (EDA), and has heard the difficulties and frustrations of numerous other carers. This book is shot with these heart-rending accounts. This in itself is of great interest and is invaluable as a source of emotional validation, comfort and support to other carers and gives an opportunity for those involved in the management of eating disorders to see the other side of the drama, the "Noises Off". There are also some poignant details of how professionals can wound and render carers guilty, frustrated, emotionally paralysed and helpless.

This book offers much more than a vivid description of a carer's experience. It is perhaps Gráinne's background, experience or part of her personality, which has meant she has not been content with experiencing and understanding alone. Rather her active problem-solving mentality has gone out searching for answers and solutions. As such she has forged for herself a pathway into the role of an "expert carer".

The Department of Health recommends the introduction of user-led self-management for chronic disease in all areas of the NHS by 2007 (DoH, 2001). The idea is that many patients could develop the skills to become expert in managing their own disease. Anorexia nervosa is a chronic illness, and so would fall into such a remit. However, because of its onset during adolescence or young adulthood the concept of expert carer is probably as appropriate as that of expert patient. This is particularly so because we know that people with an eating disorder themselves have mixed feelings about recovery.

The evidence on which the concept of an "expert carer" was developed in Stanford, CA. Kate Lorig led a research programme which found that training people who have chronic illnesses such as rheumatoid arthritis or diabetes in the management of their own illnesses, so that they become experts, increases the quality of life and overall outcome. Currently in the UK projects are under way in manic–depressive psychosis and diabetes. Kate Lorig's course, which has been used across the world, has six consecutive weekly training sessions each of 2.5 hours. This training is supplemented with patient-orientated self-help books. This book by Gráinne Smith is an excellent cornerstone for the development of this concept within eating disorders, as it provides an excellent carer-led manual.

Our experience from hosting the National Carers Conferences for Eating Disorders jointly with the Eating Disorders Association is that carers are desperate for knowledge, information, skills and resources to help them manage the day-to-day problems, which arise as part of living with someone with an eating disorder.

Research has shown that the longer the delay between the onset of the illness and active treatment the less chance there is of a good outcome (Reas et al., 2000). Family members and other carers are in the prime position to ensure that early intervention is a reality rather than an optimistic fantasy. Furthermore, families and carers can maximize the effectiveness of all treatments. Thus this book will be an invaluable contribution to all treatments for eating disorders. It can serve to take the sting of guilt and blame from the diagnosis and ensure that the process of recovering from an eating disorder takes place in the context of a collaborative effort of all those concerned.

Professionals working with people with eating disorders have recognized that specialized skills and expertise are essential for working with this client group. For example, specialized forms of psychotherapy (Dare et al., 2001) and specialized services (Nielsen et al., 1998) are associated with a better outcome. It follows that carers also need special skills.

Gráinne has succeeded in distilling the specific problems and solutions that carers face. Therefore, I hope that the book will serve as a source of inspiration for all other eating disorder carers to become "experts". Also I hope that it can break down some of the barriers between patient, carer and professional. It is all too easy for the professional to place him or herself on a pedestal offering wisdom and expertise and superior intensive care to rescue the individual from her eating disorder. Too often this is perceived as taking over where carers have failed or even stepping in to right the supposed wrongs that parents have wrought.

After reading this account I hope that professionals will develop a sense of respect and humility. How many of us could withstand such an onslaught and rejection of nurturance, the core of care?

Professor Janet Treasure
Guy's Hospital
London
13 October 2002

Preface

In autumn 1993 when my daughter finally told me that she had been diagnosed with anorexia nervosa "with elements of bulimia", I asked my GP what I could/should be doing to help. The reply was that I knew as much as the GP . . .

As a lifelong reader, I then set out to find a helpful book by someone who had experienced the illness. I searched the local library and bookshops and those within driving distance, but was handicapped by not ever having heard the phrase "an eating disorder", and therefore did not connect it with my daughter's illness, the dramatic weight loss and personality changes. It took me two years to find Eating Disorder Association (EDA) and link up what had started as a local information helpline with EDA.

For several years I continued my search, coming across all sorts of interesting, sometimes devastating, information and opinions. I found books by professionals whose writing was about patients whom they saw only in clinic and hospital settings; some of them wrote about families. I found one or two books by carers which told their own personal story, but were of little practical help beyond reassuring me that other people had been through similar situations.

In 2000 I attended the first-ever EDA Carers' Conference in London, which turned out to be a major turning point. Six months later I visited friends in Boston and spent some time in bookshops again searching for that elusive book. I wondered what was available for families coping with other life-affecting problems. It was there in Boston I found a book on how to help an alcoholic without hurting yourself (a revelation!), books on living with all sorts of other serious and chronic illnesses and disorders. But not what I was looking for ... And at last I realized that I was not going to find what I was looking for – a practical book by someone who had experience of living with all aspects of the illness.

Over the last three years I have collected together all I have learned: from reading widely in any and all areas, plus personal and work experiences that I thought just might be relevant and useful; from listening to many other family members talking about common problems in eating disorders and difficulties in coping; and from listening to and discussions with professionals who feel that families can play an important part in either supporting and maintaining the illness – or helping motivate sufferers toward the long road to fighting against eating disorders.

I hope what I have learned will be of practical use to families and other carers.

February 2003

Acknowledgements

I would like to say thank you to all the many carers I have talked to over the last few years, who have allowed me to share in their lives and stories; to the Aberdeen Eating Disorder Service, who do wonders on small resources and in difficult circumstances; to the Macduff Medical Practice; to all my many friends, who have walked alongside on the long road.

Special thanks go to Jan, Edith and Douglas for unfailing, unquestioning support in the darkest days; to Janice, who answered questions, gave me information and listened; to Margaret, who gave me hope; to Vivien Ward and Lesley Valerio at Wiley, who had faith; to Janet Treasure and Ulrike Schmidt for their interest and encouragement; and to Ian McIlwain, who said, "Get a life!" And I did.

Part I

Healing is a matter of time, but it is sometimes also a matter of opportunity.

Hippocrates (460–400 BC)

Introductions

Beginning ...

My life was opening up, I had lots of friends and an improving social life, a job that gave a lot of satisfaction as well as hard work, and I began to plan for my own future ... Work abroad for a children's charity? Write full-time? Move house?

I felt I'd come through some very tough times (some day if you have a spare week or so, I'll tell you my life story!), but my horizons were expanding, growing and I was looking forward ... then Anorexia came, uninvited, to visit my home.

Just a few years ago in 1993 I was living alone – my daughter married, my son working in Glasgow. At 48, I was working full time at a high-profile, high-energy, high-stress job (primary head teacher). Having brought up my kids from an early age on one teacher's salary, for the first time in my life I was enjoying having some money at the end of a month and had bought one or two luxuries, total unnecessaries, trying hard to get over the Scots prudence that says *Save*.

Having survived various teenage traumas, both my children seemed happy with their respective life choices. I felt I'd put into practice my strong belief in teaching a mixture of rights, responsibilities and respect for others. From an early age they were both expected to take responsibility in keeping our home, and their own rooms in particular, reasonably clean and tidy (our views of "reasonably clean and tidy" often differed – which led to me keeping their bedroom doors shut rather than look at the clutter!!). Each week I listed the chores that had to be done and asked which they'd prefer to do ... in their rush to avoid the ones they hated, they volunteered for the ones they regarded a bit more favourably, at least taking a couple of chores off my shoulders. Despite a few grumbles, they saw the fairness of helping around the house, which made the environment better for all of us. From the time they could count, they helped set the table for meals and from 12 years onward they cooked a weekday meal once a week. As they also got to choose what that meal was, they seemed happy to learn to cook at the same time as making a valuable contribution to the running of the house. (Especially at the beginning, it did mean that sometimes we ate sausages and beans rather more often than I would have preferred ...)

Training our children to be able to cope in the Big Bad World out there is an important part of being a parent as well as loving them, and I thought I'd done an OK job in bringing up my children. OK. Not brilliant – I could think of several things I felt had been mistakes along the way, but I'd always loved them, demonstrated that love often with hugs and cuddles as well as bedtime stories, games and so on, encouraged them in their individual strengths, tried to help them with things they weren't so good at. If they did their best that was good enough.

My son seemed to grow through the teenage years as he had done everything else, with good humour (and an increase in his accustomed untidiness and lack of organization), but major rows with my daughter had been part of the picture at that stage, as she stayed out until 3 or 4 in the morning and refused to even look at homework, let alone do it. But those days were now past and she appeared happy in her marriage at 19 to the boy she'd gone out with since she was 13 (the reason she had wanted to stay out at night). Unfortunately, that marriage, so much looked forward to, was a very unhappy experience and two years later Jay asked to return home. Unknown to me, Anorexia and Bulimia also came to stay.

At that time, they were just words on the edge of my vocabulary, I had never heard the phrase "an eating disorder", so I did not recognize Anorexia or Bulimia when they entered my house. I look back in incredulity at my complete ignorance and at the very steep learning curve I faced. But that ignorance was *definitely* bliss . . .

If you have picked up this book because you are a carer and have also met Anorexia and possibly Bulimia too in your home, I hope what I have written will be helpful – it is a summary of what I have learned the hard way since first meeting Anorexia and her pal. My heart and thoughts are with you on the long road.

If you are a sufferer, I know you will recognize the pain and misery inflicted by the illness, and hope you find the help you need to fight off the attentions of Anorexia and Bulimia.

If you are a professional who works with people who develop eating disorders, I hope you will read it with compassion for the carers who struggle to cope, as well as for sufferers who live in a dark, unhappy world.

And if simple curiosity has made you pick this book up, if you have never had personal experience of the devastating effects on family and friends as well as those who suffer from anorexia or bulimia nervosa, be thankful, very very thankful. And perhaps say a little prayer that whatever causes anorexia nervosa – despite hundreds of years of debate and research no one really knows – does not enter or affect your own family.

First introductions . . .

In 1994 when my daughter asked if she could move back home, I agreed – but made a few extra house rules to go with those that had applied before she married. The new rules mainly concerned television: I prefer reading, music or radio. I am very choosy about programmes and will happily spend whole evenings without watching it. I knew my daughter liked the TV on as a companion. No matter how well behaved the children, working as I did in a school meant noise – bells, voices, feet. And constant communication. I had enjoyed the silence after work during my daughter's two-year marriage, so when she returned to live at home I said the

TV should not go on after my return from work until I felt like it. She brought home a small set for her room – and we got along much better than we did in her teens! Having been responsible for organizing and running a house for two years Jay had developed more appreciation for the work involved and she was much happier and more willing to do a share of the housework than she ever had been before. After discussions, we settled on a split of chores. Since then Jay has faithfully hoovered the main rooms and cleaned the bathroom, taken her weekly turns *whatever* else was happening in life, at washing dishes (in our house, whoever cooks does not do dishes) and recycling.

She decided to diet, having put on a bit of weight during her marriage. She told me that, with her husband away a lot at work, she often nibbled in the evening. To my eye, she didn't need to, but Jay wasn't happy with her weight and felt it was important to be slimmer. Later that year she met an Interesting Man who felt she was an Interesting Woman. The relationship developed rapidly, and at weekends I rarely saw her as she waved an airy cheerio and disappeared with IM. Obviously happy, she glowed as she lost weight and exercised. She lost the weight she wanted to, enjoyed all the attention and was very flattered when she was asked to do some modelling. A very attractive youngster, Jay now looked absolutely stunning.

In spring 1995 I began to notice that the weight was still falling off and Jay was exercising even more. Each evening I could hear the exercise bike going in her room as she "cycled" miles and miles, then she did hundreds of sit-ups. Never a keen exerciser – walking the dog is quite enough! – I watched her dedication and stamina with amazement.

Over the next few months I suggested several times that the dieting had gone far enough, she really didn't need to lose any more. Each time I was dismissed as fussing. I never needed to complain about the TV being on – but the drone of the exercise bike in the ever-longer sessions was a constant irritation. When I complained, I got a very short answer.

Hindsight is a wonderful thing – these are classic symptoms of early anorexia. Would things have been different, would the course of the illness have been any shorter or taken a different course had I previously met Anorexia? I'll never know.

Anorexia moves in ...

In summer 1995 I looked forward to visiting my sister in France. The tickets were bought, my suitcase half-packed, when Jay told me that IM had "finished with her". There were no explanations and I didn't like to pry, Jay would tell me in her own time and when she was ready, as she always had in the past over what was happening in her life. But I could see how very unhappy she was. Jay assured me she would be fine in the fortnight I was away on holiday, not to worry, she would be working and that would take her mind off things. I should go, she knew how much I had looked forward to seeing my sister. As I hugged her goodbye at the airport I thought how thin she looked, thin rather than slim ...

... and two weeks later a walking skeleton met me. On one of the rare, really hot days in NE Scotland, Jay was dressed in cut-off shorts and a brief top and people were staring at her as we walked to the car. I had difficulty taking my eyes from the huge joints standing out from stick legs as she changed gear, the rings sliding up and down bony fingers on the steering wheel.

I thought she had cancer. When my father died many years before, he'd been very emaciated.

Remembering Jay's previous cross dismissal of my concerns, I hesitantly brought up my continuing worries about her weight. *Perhaps*, I said, *perhaps she should go to the doctor ...*

I've been to the doctor! He's done tests and there's nothing wrong with me!

Perhaps there are other tests ...

Oh Mum, do stop fussing!

Similar conversations took place over the next weeks. Sitting across from me at the table, Jay appeared to eat normally. We were both out working, so I didn't know exactly what she ate during the day – but I saw her making up a good packed lunch each night. *Cancer ... what else could it be? Cancer can run in families, I knew that ... Cancer ...* By now I was sick with worry and dread. Jay's face was all bone with skin stretched tight, eyes dark and staring, arms and legs like sticks, her hip bones stood out and clothes were hanging off her. She proudly told me one night that instead of the size 12 she'd worn at the time of her wedding, she was now a size 6 and could get into children's clothing. When I held her now, it was like holding a sack of bones; I became afraid to hug her properly for fear she would break.

September brought a visit from my friends, William and Jess. Jess waited until Jay had gone outside with William to smoke (another rule of the house!), then asked if Jay had seen a doctor ... Jess recognized all the signs, as she had a colleague who suffered from ... anorexia ...

The following week, the phone rang while we were sitting at the table. It was our GP, asking to speak to Jay. I handed the phone over and returned to eating. Then I saw Jay's face change. Later that evening she said she had something to tell me. During her marriage she had begun to have problems with food, eating out of boredom and unhappiness. Her husband had told her, among other things, that she was fat and ugly and that he'd slept with other women. When she found him with another girl was when she'd asked if she could come home. But her food problems had continued ... she'd started to diet, then found she could lose weight faster if she got rid of anything she swallowed ... and now she couldn't stop.

The doctor had indeed done tests, just as Jay had told me, everything he could think of in fact. Eventually, he had diagnosed anorexia nervosa, with elements of bulimia. On the phone earlier that evening he'd told Jay that her potassium level was so low that, at 23, she was at serious risk of a heart attack. Sitting holding her that evening, we both wept, Jay with fear that she might die. My own fear of the same was mixed with helplessness and horror at my own blindness – how had Jay managed to get rid of all the food she'd eaten in front of me? How could I possibly not have known what she was doing? It was only with hindsight that I remembered that Jay with her fondness for all the TV soaps, left the table after our meal to go upstairs to her room to watch. *I know you don't like the programme and you don't want the TV on just now anyway, do you Mum? I'll watch it upstairs ...*

Now of course I know that both Anorexia and Bulimia are very clever at covering their activities, and giving plausible reasons for frequent visits to the bathroom.

Later, much much later, a long way through the journey with the twin demons, my daughter told me that during my holiday in France with my sister, she had eaten nothing at all. Nothing. Drinking coffee had been her only sustenance. It was only when Dr Brooker said she was putting her life at risk by her eating behaviour, that she had begun to realize that the condition was serious. And she might die if she continued with the behaviour.

But Jay couldn't stop – Anorexia and Bulimia were firmly in control and the behaviour was compulsive.

Arrivals

Dialogue

A skeleton walks held erect by stalks,
by strings of sinew, huge knees on view, jutting bone.
Each step's a marathon.

Don't fuss. Get lost,
leave me be, I'm fine.

Bones strain from paper skin
stretched taut, as scraped by a knife.
Rings slither, slide on fingers
grimly holding onto life.

No, I won't. Here at eating
now I draw the line.

Brilliant, dark with pain eyes stare
past sustenance of body, soul,
see only black, bleak, lonely, bare,
see only night and melanchole.

Can't you see how gross I am?
So fat and overweight?

All around the voices speak, echoing daily-day,
whispering, hissing, sighing,
deceitful words to kill the mind,
insinuating, clever, lying.

I mustn't eat, I don't deserve
the food that's on my plate.

Hunger makes me strong to fight the ones who'd make me big.
Controlling food is all I own. Give way? I'm just a pig.
You can't love me, why do you lie?
Tasting, feeling, means I've failed. I really want to die.

Most guests arrive with an invitation, some being very welcome friends of long standing, others more recent acquaintances. Usually, their stay will be enjoyable with discussions of topics of mutual interest, shared meals and perhaps some outings. Usually, guests stay for an agreed length of time before leaving; you wave goodbye and resume your day-to-day activities.

Occasionally, however, someone turns up unexpectedly and gains admittance under false pretences. Only at a later date the host will realize that the guest installed under their roof and making themselves comfortable is not all they appeared. Unusual and upsetting behaviour has affected the family balance, the daily flow has changed, and family members begin to feel uneasy, although at times they may not be able to pinpoint exactly when changes began. With an unwelcome, but tenacious, guest it may be extremely difficult to show them the door and effect an eviction.

Anorexia has arrived and has made her presence felt, but you're not sure quite when she moved in. Possibly Bulimia has come along too, but maybe not. Weight loss after illness is one starting point, but often an eating disorder starts with some sort of diet or food restriction, perhaps after a throwaway remark by a friend about losing a few pounds, perhaps following a broken romance, perhaps after bullying at school, (although you may or may not have been aware of any of these at the time). Then the diet has been enhanced by exercise – running, extra hockey, cycling, sit-ups, aerobics ... At first your daughter or son felt fantastic, was on a high and was delighted with all the compliments. Then the few pounds became stones. The exercise has become compulsive and the weight loss dramatic. Now she doesn't feel so good, the exercise is much more of an effort, she just doesn't have the same amount of energy, she feels the cold much more than she used to ...

At intervals you have tentatively suggested that the dieting need not be continued – weight was already well below that recommended for height and bones were showing through fragile skin. You speak of your concerns tentatively, hesitantly, because the response is sharp. *Stop fussing! None of your business! Leave me alone, you just don't understand!* And Anorexia can be very intimidating – and sound quite reasonable – in defence of privacy.

Perhaps you have noticed that very little food is being eaten, although food is pressed on others. Perhaps Bulimia has made the discovery that weight can be lost much quicker if whatever she can't avoid swallowing is followed by vomiting. Perhaps Anorexia has taken to wearing baggy clothes to "hide her disgusting body" or perhaps her aim is to get into ever-smaller clothes sizes. What can't be hidden are the hollows under eyes and the skeletal fingers, the jutting shoulder and hip bones.

Even then Anorexia argues that she is far too fat, that she is in fact quite gross. *Just look at her disgusting tummy, her bum, for proof!! Look, look in the mirror and see what she sees* ... but Anorexia's view in the mirror, in front of which she spends much anxious time, is distorted. Where others see bones standing out through clothes, she sees fat; where others see hollows she sees roundness. And drives him or herself on to even greater efforts in self-starvation.

Not only is Anorexia's view in the mirror distorted, relationships are likewise changed as self-esteem is lost in the focus on food, the hourly, daily battle to stop giving in to the body's demands for sustenance. Reality retreats as Anorexia takes over. Where concern is intended, Anorexia hears only interference. Where love is expressed, there is disbelief – both Bulimia and Anorexia think no one could possibly love someone so fat, so gross, so lacking in self-discipline.

Efforts to enlist the help of a doctor are likely to be dismissed by Anorexia, and GPs are unlikely to listen to the worries of parents. Parents who, in their attempts to alert the medical profession and try to explain their anxiety as they watch their child become a walking skeleton, are in fact most likely to be labelled – and dismissed – as overprotective, fussing and interfering, by GPs and other professionals.

Then at last, at long last, Anorexia has admitted that perhaps there is a problem, but isn't sure what she can do. Bulimia is not at all sure about speaking to anyone about the problem; they might not understand, they might criticize, they might try to stop her losing weight. Even in admitting the possibility of a problem, Anorexia and Bulimia find it difficult to contemplate the idea of changing, but at last summon enough courage to talk to a friend, perhaps a trusted teacher, perhaps her mother. Perhaps that friend, whoever it is, whether within or outside the family, finally manages to persuade Anorexia or Bulimia to speak to a GP.

Possibly Anorexia or Bulimia even goes on her own. Frequently the GP is very positive about the future – after all, Anorexia appears to be a sensible person. But while one part of her mind takes in all the information about Body Mass Index (the relationship between height and weight), about healthy eating, about the need her body has for balanced nutrition to allow her heart and other organs to function, Anorexia's mind is planning how to continue losing weight. **Anorexia's reality is different from anyone else's – not for Anorexia ordinary amounts of food to feed an ordinary body, she can thrive on much much less than other people. Can't she?**

By this time, family and friends are really worried. Attempts to persuade, to cajole, to humour, to tempt, have all met with failure. Where before they perhaps guessed at cancer or some wasting disease, now they suspect or know the truth – Anorexia has taken over. Some friends move on, drift away, unable to cope or rejected by Anorexia. Family relationships hit a new low. In the past there have been ups and downs, now Down is the norm as everyone tiptoes around trying to say and do the right thing only to find there is no right thing – it changes daily. Screaming tempers are often heard as Anorexia refuses all well-meaning attempts at help as well as any inadvertent trespassing on her emotional pain. Laughter seems to have flown out of the window. The further Anorexia retreats from reality the more helpless and despairing the family become. This is when many family members – often brothers and sisters, sometimes fathers – give up and leave, causing even more distress to those left trying to cope, and this is when many parents find they can no longer cope with other life stresses as well as what is happening at home. Frequently, the main carer, often but not always a distraught mother, gives up her own life outside the home, including work, unable to cope with all the demands 24 hours a day. (In common with many others I have talked to on the helpline and at meetings, I got to that stage and gave up my job.)

With no help, no support and frequently little information, many parents are prey to feelings of guilt and shame as they try to come to terms with displays of temper, lying and cheating in their own family. They thought they had brought up their children to be honest, to respect others, to behave in accordance with the rules of society, and now here, within their own family, Anorexia – especially if her pal Bulimia has come with her – is behaving in a very different way.

And, of course, families become aware of the stigma that often attaches to mental illness. Frequently, long-standing family friends melt away, perhaps uncertain how to respond, perhaps unable to cope with another's distress over a long spell. Worst of all, not only do parents watch in agony as their previously healthy child turns into a walking skeleton and their child retreats into tantrums and screaming rages that they thought long past, they also have to cope with wondering what they could possibly have done wrong to cause someone they love to want to actively starve themselves.

In our society, Fault and Blame are constant companions and parents worry that something they did at some time in the past might have caused Anorexia to appear:

- *Is it because my child had to move home/school at the wrong time?*
- *Is it because she was the youngest and we all spoiled her a bit?*
- *Is it because as the oldest in the family she was expected to take too much responsibility?*
- *Is it because we were too strict? Or too lax? Or too demanding?*
- *Is it because we left her with a childminder before she went to school?*
- *We've both always worked hard to give our children a good education and standard of living, is it because we worked too-long hours and she felt neglected?*
- *Did we somehow give the wrong examples?*
- *Is it because we sent all our children, including our son, to boarding school?*
- *Is it because we moved several times because of my husband's job?*
- *Is it because we made her go to school when she hated it so much at the beginning? She hated it so much, we moved her to another school, then later on when she hated that one, a different school again . . . We tried to do our best . . . We only wanted what was best but maybe it was all wrong . . .*

All these thoughts and feelings are endorsed and multiplied by articles and books written in the era before the discovery of the role of genes and other factors, the era when parents, especially mothers, were frequently held responsible for the ills of their children. This was true not only in eating disorders, but in autism, Asperger's Syndrome, schizophrenia ... On the helpline and at meetings it is one of the most frequently-asked questions – *Is it because ...?*

> *Calling Anorexia an eating disorder is like calling cancer a cough.*
>
> Professor Arthur Crisp (June 2000)

Anorexia, whether operating alone or alongside Bulimia, has a devastating effect not only on the lives of those who suffer from this serious mental illness but also on their families. Families desperately want to know what they can do to help, want to know how best to support their relative. Their worst fear is that something they are doing might indeed be making things worse ... but "where can they find help or guidance?" and "why is it so difficult to find support, even information?" Many GPs know little about eating disorders – their training gives only a very bare outline and they may meet a case of anorexia nervosa infrequently. Bulimia hides activities as much as possible and only very reluctantly will talk to anyone, a friend or a family member, let alone a doctor. Other doctors, with specialist knowledge, seem secretive about giving information, perhaps because they find it difficult to give what they feel is very bad news, perhaps because they have reservations about the reactions of parents to talking about the worst features of the illnesses. Perhaps others feel that ignoring carers is somehow protecting their patients. Whatever the reasons, lack of information adds to the sadness and frustration of families.

Finding the following statement at least gave me an answer to why this situation has continued for so long:

> *Practitioners and treatment systems have not only failed to offer family education, but in too many cases they have intentionally avoided any communication with families except for collecting background information about the circumstances of the disorder. Family members' questions, their very natural attempts to obtain information about what is wrong with their relative and what they can do*

to help, have been carefully deflected or ignored by the treating professionals. Traditionally, this failure to communicate with family members was the deliberate policy of many mental health facilities. Although its effects were cruel and often damaging to the patient and family, the policy was considered necessary for effective treatment. It was based on a model of mental illness in which recovery was viewed as evolving from a therapeutic alliance between the patient and therapist. In this model, it was felt that any communication with family members would be experienced as a breach of trust by the patient and would gravely interfere with progress in treatment. Most models, in fact, viewed the family as a source of "toxins" rather than help ...

(Mueser and Gingerich, 1994)

... If doctors truly believed that people with mental health and other problems were always the result of poor parenting, then obviously they believed that excluding the influences of the family would benefit their patients. There are, unhappily, indeed families who cause hurt to or abuse their children. Sometimes the damage is done through circumstances, such as a job that involves frequent moves, when children are uprooted and then find it difficult to form relationships; sometimes a parent has communication or other difficulties themselves that affect the children; and worst of all, there are occasionally people who deliberately abuse their children.

Unfortunately, the view of the family as "toxic" was extended to all parents and families, whatever the circumstances.

When Jay began to lose dramatic amounts of weight I initially thought she had cancer. **If the diagnosis had indeed been cancer as I feared, a care plan would have been offered** ...

After years of searching for a care plan; of experiencing all the same pain and misery, utter despair and helplessness other parents, partners and friends have described to me; of searching for information only to find along with it the idea that I was viewed by some professionals as responsible for my daughter's illness; of finding by trial and error (many errors!) what helped my daughter – and me –

I now know that there is no one care plan that will work for everyone.

I now know there are no easy answers for families coping with a visit from Anorexia and Bulimia. Although there are similarities in behaviour, every case is individual with individual features.

3

Prepare for a long road

Your help is needed and is critical for your daughter's health.

Janet Treasure (1997)

Recognizing anorexia . . . how can you be sure that your daughter is not suffering from some other physical illness? Other illnesses too can cause weight loss. You may have noticed changes over some time, but only at a later date realized that they may be significant, by which time your daughter has lost a large amount of weight and Anorexia, possibly aided and abetted by Bulimia, has taken over. Both Anorexia and Bulimia are very skilful at hiding what they are doing, at sounding quite reasonable when they state why they are not seeing friends, why frequent visits to the bathroom are necessary. Many parents, when finally recognizing the scale of the problem, wonder why they didn't become aware much earlier. In my own case, I was utterly blind. When Jay immediately went upstairs after eating a hearty meal to her room "to watch TV", I thought nothing of it. After all, I didn't watch the soaps, didn't want the TV on where I was sitting and imagined it was thoughtful of her to spare me all the melodrama by watching TV in her bedroom. Had I known that before watching the first of the soaps she visited the toilet, I doubt if at that time I would have wondered at it. It is only on becoming aware of Bulimia's activities that I, along with most other people, realize why all the food consumed is not translated into a healthy body.

Here are some common signs that may alert you to Anorexia and/or Bulimia:

- Loss of weight, possibly (not always) disguised by wearing baggy clothes.
- Possibly avoiding eating with the family, giving plausible reasons (e.g., she has eaten earlier or will eat later when she feels hungry).
- When she does eat with the family, she piles her plate with salad or vegetables and avoids anything containing carbohydrates or fat.
- She may cut everything on her plate into tiny pieces and push it around rather than eat.
- High level of physical activity, can't sit still, hyperactivity.
- Very bright eyes, enlarged pupils.
- A change of physical activity from team games to solitary exercise such as running.
- Difficulties with friends.
- Change of mood – she will become more irritable, tearful and impatient (to put it mildly).
- Possible binge eating when her control breaks and her body cries out for nourishment – large amounts of food may disappear.
- After bingeing, she may vomit.
- She may use laxatives as a way of getting rid of food.
- Frequent visits to the bathroom during and after eating.
- Possibly feeling the cold.
- Eventually, lethargy as energy is depleted because of lack of food.
- Changes in hair quality.
- Poor concentration.
- Minor problems appear insurmountable; mountains are made out of molehills.

Anorexia and Bulimia frequently appear in the teenage years, and any one of these signs alone might be explained by common teenage behaviour. **Several of the signs together may spell anorexia, with or without bulimia nervosa**.

Ever since anorexia nervosa was first described in the late 1600s, doctors have been arguing about the causes; many theories have been developed, many discarded. One thing that is agreed is that, once established, the illness is extremely difficult to treat, given the patients' resistance to doing the one thing that would help – even save her life – and that is to eat. Overcoming Anorexia's obstinacy at attempts to help, and her anger at anyone who suggests change, are major challenges and will not happen overnight. A particular problem is her frequent rage at family members who in their anxiety express their concern or try various ways to get her to take food. *My daughter has been sectioned because she just doesn't recognize how ill she is. The doctors said she would die if she wasn't in hospital. Now she hates me and is really hostile when I try to speak to her – she blames me for her being hospitalized. But the doctors say she'd be dead otherwise* (EDA helpline).

It is the long, frustrating battle with motivation that causes great difficulties for carers, families and doctors alike, leading, therefore, to the long long road that both sufferers and carers have to follow.

At best, Anorexia will take over for months; at worst for many years. Bulimia may not accompany Anorexia but frequently does. There are unfortunately patients whose lives have been so blighted by both Anorexia and Bulimia that they die either by suicide or through developing physical problems such as mineral imbalances caused by lack of particular nutrients in their diet (e.g., lack of potassium can lead to heart problems). Sadly, in some cases the best efforts of highly-qualified and experienced doctors as well as loving families are no match for Anorexia.

One of the most difficult aspects of the illnesses, not only for families but also for many doctors, is that there is no medical treatment, such as medication or an operation, that might help. Treatment has been developed by observation over long years of what works. Parents, who have watched a child becoming emaciated, not surprisingly often feel ill with worry and anxiety and want doctors to find an answer and a cure as quickly as possible. It is difficult to accept that doctors, with all their modern technology, drugs and treatments, may be rendered as helpless as parents themselves in the face of the determined resistance of Anorexia and Bulimia to accept help, even to accept that she has a problem.

Over these past centuries it has been found that different treatments have some success with some patients. Several doctors have gradually developed treatment based on active collaboration between therapist, sufferer and family that has been successful in many cases. However, resources are very limited. One positive step parents might take is to lobby MPs for better resources, including training for GPs and other healthcare professionals, who may only meet Anorexia infrequently and have many other priorities.

At least the extreme thinness of Anorexia cannot be hidden from medical eyes. But unfortunately Bulimia, working alone without Anorexia, is clever at hiding her activities. She can even maintain a "normal" weight while presenting a bright face and is so reluctant to discuss health problems, resulting from repeated vomiting or use of laxatives, that unsuspecting doctors may treat patients for various ailments without guessing that the problems are not caused, for instance, by bowel problems, but by heavy use of laxatives.

Specialist services are scattered and often patchy, all of which adds to the misery and frustration families feel. Not only have Anorexia and Bulimia argued forcefully against all attempts at logic and intervention, when they are finally persuaded at long long last of the need for professional help to overcome problems, more valuable time is lost in trying to find someone who knows how to help. If there is a long wait over months for an appointment, both Bulimia and Anorexia may have changed their mind about attending ... And all the time the illness is getting a firmer grip and family life is becoming more and more fraught, disintegrating under the stress Anorexia and Bulimia bring with them.

Anorexia and Bulimia have no scruples. They will lie, cheat, manipulate everyone within their range. At times solemn promises will be made to a distraught mother or father that yes, she will eat – and then hide or get rid of the few mouthfuls. While fighting for control over eating, she will also try to control whoever and whatever she can, playing off one family member against the other. Family relationships by this time have frequently deteriorated into chaos as everyone tries to work out a way of coping with

and possibly helping someone whom they love but whose personality is totally changed.

It is difficult and painful to accept the aggression and rejection
that frequently accompany these illnesses – when family members
only want to help. Parents, siblings, grandparents and friends may
respond by trying to ignore the problems, by expressing disgust,
by staying out as much as possible, by trying to force Anorexia to
eat by threatening, by trying to cajole and persuade, by losing their
temper in the face of total intransigence ... or a combination of all.
Trying to prevent Bulimia from carrying on with activities that are
not only disgusting for family members but are affecting Bulimia's
health is just as difficult and leads to many family battles.

Trying to keep calm, state your concerns and avoid shouting
back in the face of irrational temper, screaming and shouting is
extremely difficult. Saints have been known to crack ...

- *Remember* – Anorexia and Bulimia's thinking is not clear, perceptions are distorted and all their reactions are to an altered
  reality that is not yours. Denial of problems is part of the
  illness – the more Anorexia and Bulimia say there is no
  problem the more help is needed. When, just after diagnosis,
  it was suggested that Jay should be in hospital, her reaction
  was "No way!" – and to sever all connection with treatment
  (which, of course, deepened the black hole for me as far as
  knowing what to do was concerned).
- *Remember* that Anorexia has come to stay in your daughter's
  place.
- *Remember* that Anorexia is in emotional turmoil and is deeply
  unhappy. If you don't understand her behaviour, no more
  does she and she is probably very frightened.
- *Remember* also that **no-one will change because they are
  told to**. Angry confrontations only lead to more entrenched
  resistance. The more you argue the less you are likely to persuade of the need for change.

Do you remember the story of the Sun and the Wind, who had a
competition to see who could make a man take off his coat? When
the Wind raged and blew as hard as possible, the man not only did
not take off his coat he did up all the buttons and turned up the

collar ... Then the Sun shone calmly and gently, and kept on shining. Eventually, the man relaxed, undid the buttons, opened his collar – and finally took off his coat. But it took time for the man to relax enough, to believe ...

According to psychologists Prochaska and Di Clemente, there are five stages people go through when deciding to change any aspect of life:

- *Precontemplation* – not ready to recognize the need for change.
- *Contemplation* – thinking toward the possibility of change.
- *Preparation* – worry about what will happen if they change.
- *Action* – individuals commit to change and initiate changes. Lots of support and encouragement is needed.
- *Maintenance* – change is continued.

To Anorexia, the fear of change is quite terrifying – with all perceptions distorted, she would rather stay locked in her games, habits and rituals than risk change. This is where families can help. Don't listen to protests that it is none of your business – **Anorexia is affecting your life and therefore it is your business**.

Try to remain calm in the face of provocation (not easy!), encourage any positive steps no matter how small. And try to find calmer moments when you can say, "I love you very much, but I don't like it when you ..." (More of this later.) One major problem for Anorexia is that in her distorted world, she cannot hear or see expressions of love. She needs constant reassurance at the same time as having it pointed out that other people are worthy of respect, other people have rights too.

All of this takes time. Several steps forward may be taken – then backward; several false starts may be taken on the road to change before progress is consolidated. And each step may take months, even years. Try to keep hope for the future – again, not easy – and keep in mind that with a lot of work some day your beloved daughter will return. At first, your daughter may return for short spells only to be overtaken by Anorexia again – and this may happen many times. Eventually, Anorexia's visits may become fewer and last for shorter periods.

So families must prepare for a long road ahead, to help and support each other as well as their daughter. If possible, try to meet with other carers. And if at all possible try to meet a former sufferer. Talking with people who have recovered and are now living ordinary lives, hearing what helped them fight off the attentions of Anorexia, is wonderful and gives hope for the future.

4

Living with the volcano

Complete unpredictability, hostility and the aggression encountered by anyone living with Anorexia and Bulimia were identified as some of the most difficult aspects of trying to cope (EDA, 2000). Carers remember ordinary family life BA (Before Anorexia) with ordinary ups and downs, family meals and celebrations, outings and holidays, happy times and squabbles. Now it seems that no matter what happens, Anorexia's spectacular temper is lying just below the surface, ready to erupt and bombard whoever is in the path of fallout. And the nearer you are, the more likely you are to suffer.

> *Every time I try to talk to my daughter about the mess she leaves in the bathroom, the fact that again there is no food left for anyone's breakfast, she explodes and starts screaming about how no one understands. We do try to understand and can see how unhappy she is, but life at home is becoming intolerable – everyone tries to tiptoe around and not upset her but no matter what we do it's not right. My youngest son is 16 and stays out later and later; he says he can't stand living here any more. Sometimes talking about ordinary things, nothing to do with food or her behaviour, even trying to ignore bad behaviour, can lead*

*to an explosion. My husband is talking about leaving ...
and I don't think I can cope much longer.*
                    A carer, EDA helpline (October 2000)

Carers frequently describe the sense of complete rejection they
feel, each story different and yet similar. Parents don't need
anyone else to point the finger of blame – they are very good at it
already without any outside help. These crushing feelings of guilt,
of somehow not being able to protect their family member from
pain and distress, of not knowing what to do are regular features of
life for people who care. And Anorexia and Bulimia are expert at
using those feelings ...

Unpredictability is another feature of the illness carers find
most difficult to cope with and adds to family bewilderment.
One day while she is cooking she wants the kitchen door left
open, saying if it is closed she feels shut in; next day when it is
left open as instructed, she wants it shut. If you offer to make
coffee for her along with others, it is not to her taste; don't offer
and you don't care.

Sometimes Anorexia goes out for a while without you
knowing, and there is no reaction at all to something you
thought would cause problems. Perhaps you have been braced to
tackle the subject of Bulimia leaving enough food for other
members of the family for breakfast. You have rehearsed what
you want to say, your heart is racing with apprehension because
of Anorexia's previous aggressive reactions. "OK!", your daughter
says quite reasonably. You feel a flood of relief. What were you
worried about?! So you relax a bit ... until the next time there is no
food left – but this time Anorexia explodes. You go through the
same scene all over again – but the reaction is different this time.
Anorexia has ended her break away.

Anorexia's whole life is focused around food, her own and that
of others. She may spend hours talking about food, about recipes,
about the calorie value of various items. She may love to cook for
and watch others eat, while denying herself food. Anorexia feels
that her denial is a triumph over the needs of her body, and everything – no matter how remote the connection – may be seen by
Anorexia as an attempt to break the self-imposed starvation, an
attempt to change a chosen way of living. No matter how reason-

able a comment or request, it may be seen by Anorexia, whose grasp on logic is lost, as critical of her in some way.

If Bulimia accompanies Anorexia, Anorexia is utterly disgusted and very distressed by what she sees as a breakdown of self-control. Each time Bulimia takes over and binges, frantic attempts are made by Anorexia to purge the body of all food, get rid of all the "evil" sustenance, evidence of greed. In Anorexia's mind, Fit equals Good and Fat equals Greed – but all sense of proportion of what is actually fat or greed is completely gone.

As Anorexia struggles for control of her own life she frequently tries to control those of others around her by manipulating, distorting or twisting the truth, frequently playing one family member off against another. Unless family members become aware of this and sit down together to discuss what is happening – and this in itself can be difficult given what Anorexia has been saying to each individual about the others! – Anorexia has little difficulty in maintaining her control of the family.

With distorted vision, Anorexia sees the concern of others and attempts to help as interference, sees any mention of or praise for others as proof of no love for her. Reasonable requests to respect the rights of others – perhaps to finding the bathroom in a clean state – are seen as an intrusion into Bulimia's privacy. Most of these requests are quite sensible (e.g., trying to find ways of getting Anorexia to eat when she is very obviously starving) to everyone except Anorexia.

Perhaps some of the screaming tempers are associated with a vague sense of guilt, perhaps there is some other as-yet-undiscovered reason, but whatever the cause families find living with outbursts unnerving at best, extremely distressing at worst. Life as it was BA becomes impossible, a faint memory of a time long ago and far away.

Frequently, family members simply give up and give in to whatever Anorexia or Bulimia wants at that particular moment. However, in giving in to unreasonable requests; carers lay up trouble for the future. Not to give in, to stand firm in maintaining the family rules and the right to respect of every member, is really difficult. Families, particularly the main carer, often become exhausted and some become ill themselves. Many families bankrupt themselves, physically and emotionally as well as financially, in their attempts to help Anorexia and to get help for her. **But unless Anorexia herself sees and accepts the need for change, there is little anyone can do, which of course is the most frustrating aspect of the illness.**

It is important for families to remember that their relative is being affected by "the Anorexic minx" (Treasure, 1997). When your relative is being aggressive and beyond reason, try to back off and withdraw – Anorexia is in charge and *no* one can reason with her. You can't win – no matter what you do or say will be wrong according to Anorexia and her pal – so what about a walk? At least the dog would be pleased! Or some peaceful music in a different room, or maybe book in for a massage?

It is important to think about how you approach Anorexia and Bulimia with requests. If Anorexia is making a fuss about some-thing you consider trivial, is it worth you getting angry? If she wants a door open rather than shut, or vice versa, no matter what she wanted yesterday or an hour ago, is it really worth making any comment on it at all? Easier just to shrug and shut/leave open the door. However, if Bulimia is screaming because you have mentioned that you would like food left for breakfast, perhaps you could think about that request – is it reasonable to ask this? Would you ask this of anyone else? Would you accept such aggres-sive, unpleasant behaviour from anyone else? No? Restate your request – you may have to wait for a later, quieter moment – making every effort to keep your tone calm and nonjudgmental.

Anorexia's self-esteem is very low and she will see even gentle reminders of the rights of others as a criticism. Deaf to expressions of caring, hearing only criticism, Anorexia longs for love and acceptance. It is therefore especially important to find the right words and the right moment (not easy!) to broach what may be a difficult subject. The way a request is made is often the key to a successful outcome (see Chapter 15).

Often carers are afraid that by trying to stand up to Anorexia and withstand her unreasonable behaviour they might make things worse. *You don't understand, you don't care, you don't love me. Life is not worth living – I'm going to end it all.* This may be part of the emotional blackmail employed by Anorexia and Bulimia to control all around, but it is a very real threat and sadly sometimes Anorexia is so far beyond reality and so depressed that she attempts self-harm or suicide.

All the more reason to try to keep calm, to end any potential confrontation by leaving the room or even the house for a while. Whatever the reaction, try not to be provoked into losing your own cool (Anorexia may try her best to do just that.) You may have to repeat the exercise many times over many months. Having said your piece, move on – to another topic, to another room, to read your book, to the garden. Or go for that walk. By trying to separate your daughter's behaviour from that of the Anorexic minx, it may be easier to detach your own painful feelings of rejection.

5

Horrible habits and ghastly games

Anorexia is now well established. At first, food and eating seemed to be the issue. Anorexia's whole being is focused on avoiding eating, and she will do anything, anything at all to get her way. This includes not eating at all − self-starvation − for as long as possible, pretending to eat and hiding food when it seems unavoidable to eat with others, lying about having eaten earlier or not being hungry, wild binges − which may even include eating frozen food direct from the freezer compartment − when the rigid control slips and Bulimia overpowers Anorexia and can't resist eating everything in sight, then getting rid of it.

At first, Anorexia is very lively, noticeably energetic and exercising frequently, but her body can't keep this up for long without sustenance ...

Human bodies need a certain amount of food or fuel simply to keep the major organs going − just keeping your heart beating 24 hours a day requires a lot of energy. Without proper nourishment, Anorexia's body starts to take energy away from less important functions, such as growing strong nails and hair, to concentrate on just keeping warm enough and alive! After the initial stage of compulsive and exhausting activity, to try to conserve energy and to keep warm Anorexia's body will want to spend a lot of time lying down and may grow a layer of downy hair while the hair on her head grows thinner. Teeth may be affected as well as skin condition because essential mineral elements to keep them clear and healthy are missing. There is simply not enough energy available to keep up normal life as it was known before Anorexia arrived; the compulsive activity gives way to lethargy and fatigue. Even talking takes energy, and often friends are dropped as social life is curtailed, quite apart from the fact that Anorexia finds it impossible to believe that anyone could love her or have an interest in her. Anorexia may develop rituals and obsessions to help her cope.

Without necessary nourishment, balanced vitamins and minerals, such as potassium and zinc as well as protein, carbohydrates and so on, it is not only Anorexia's body that begins to react and protest. Anorexia begins to sound irritable and bad-tempered over trivial things that never caused a problem before, and her perceptions of relationships and events change and distort as she loses the ability to think clearly and logically. One of the consequences of very low weight is depression and concentration is badly affected, causing more problems if Anorexia is expected to work at school, studying at college or university or trying to hold down a job.

As Anorexia becomes established, her family and friends find her behaviour more and more difficult and struggle to cope. Where bingeing is a problem, family members may get up or arrive home from a hard day's work or school to find no food left. No milk to go in coffee – if there is any coffee left – no bread to make a sandwich or toast, no biscuits, no cereal, no fruit. Nothing in the fridge or freezer. Cupboards are completely bare. Bulimia has been bingeing and the whole lot has gone down the loo ... which is probably in a disgusting mess.

Bulimia may also find the compulsion to binge so strong that her previous moral code is overwhelmed. She may steal money from family and friends to buy more food; she may shoplift. If friends discover what has happened – as they may well do – Anorexia's infrequent social outings may stop altogether. If family suspect or prove that Anorexia has been taking money from wallets and purses – and they may well do – trust is destroyed and may be difficult to restore. And if she is caught and accused of shoplifting – as she may well be – a court appearance may be the next step. Anorexia's and Bulimia's family feel caught in the middle of a web of deceit of nightmarish quality, with no end in sight and no idea what to do.

Bathroom and kitchen habits also deteriorate. Disgusting towels may be found lying around, toilets may be left splashed with vomit, huge numbers of toilet rolls are used every week, pans and bowls and plates are often left unwashed. If Anorexia is obsessive about her bedroom, it *may* be a model of tidiness – but in other cases where Bulimia has moved in it may be a revolting tip that smells.

Family members frequently complain loudly to the management rather than risk Anorexia's wrath, which is spectacular over trivial things – no tomato sauce left two days after stocking the cupboards? The fact that Anorexia finished the three large bottles you bought for the whole family is irrelevant to her! The temper is way over the top in the face of what is legitimate complaint. And the management – usually a distressed and despairing, frequently exhausted, mother – tries to work out what to do. Should she take the easy way out and buy more food (that is if she has any money left)? Should she be the one to clean up the kitchen, clean the toilet yet again? Many do just that, rather than risk another confrontation and Anorexia screaming. Anorexia's aggression in the face of what she sees as criticism can be really frightening.

The problem with this approach is **that by opting out of tackling the problems, by trying as far as possible to ignore them and keep the peace, the problems will only multiply**.

Anorexia's temper will grow and flourish over ever-smaller incidents anyway, whatever you do. If families try to ignore and tiptoe around the problems, Bulimia gets the message that by making life unpleasant enough she can "get away" with things and can take ever greater control over the lives of everyone around her. This does not make her happier – the guilt about what she is doing probably increases the misery and contributes to her outbursts.

To some extent Anorexia's behaviour is outwith her control. Reality has retreated and she has lost sight of the needs of others or the idea of considering them. To help Anorexia control her eating or lack of eating, the bingeing, or stealing, or shoplifting, she needs

Figure 1 A *full-blown, over-the-top, out-of-control Hairy Jamaica* (Jay's description of an anorexic rage) – scary!

someone to stand up to her and to lay down the law – the Law of Reality, the Law of the Household. It may not be what she wants, just as a child wants everything its own way and will scream, tantrum and push as far as possible to achieve its short-term wants, but without any help toward some sort of control Anorexia will simply continue to destroy all around her with hostility and aggression.

But it isn't easy to re-establish rules that have been blurred, let alone establish others that were never necessary in the past (e.g., *You will not lick your plate in front of me please! If you really have to, go into the kitchen/outside*). This is especially so when, frequently, one of Anorexia's threats is that she will commit suicide if people don't give in to what she wants – more tomato sauce, the door open or closed on whim, a particular mug or spoon, which must be remembered and may change from day to day ...

And she means it. A threat of suicide is the ultimate in emotional blackmail and of course creates fear in the hearts of family and friends. The very real fear that this time, this day, Anorexia really will carry out her threats, is what keeps many families in despair and in thrall to Anorexia's behaviour.

6

Family actions and reactions

Although anorexia can affect all ages from childhood upward, the most common age for anorexia to claim victims is in the teenage years and often brothers and sisters are a few years older or younger. While siblings may know that Anorexia and/or Bulimia is ill and suffering, it is very difficult to accept that all their parents' attention seems focused on her when they too are going through growing up problems, exams, perhaps bullying ... When they come home there may be no food left, Bulimia got there first. Pocket money sometimes disappears and no one wants to admit the problem. Everyone feels the need of attention and support – but Anorexia and Bulimia working together demand all that is going.

Family gatherings and visitors become difficult as Anorexia finds it impossible to cope with company in the house, even when she has known the people for many years. Attempts at chat with a visitor are interrupted frequently as Anorexia demands attention. Casual invitations for coffee become impossible unless coffee, biscuits and sugar are hidden, as frequently the cupboards have been cleared. Visitors frequently don't know how to react and find other things to do. Families often stop inviting friends and even family around rather than risk another embarrassing scene.

For younger family members, home doesn't feel like the place it used to be:

■ *Coming home from school one day, Sam, 9, found that Bulimia had moved into his bedroom — Mum had complained that Bulimia's bedroom was disgusting because of the smelly towels lying all over the floor, but instead of tidying it up Bulimia had moved into Sam's room. Sam felt really angry and told her to get out, but she's a lot bigger than him and horrible to her little brother; and he knew he couldn't make her get out of his room. So Sam went to Mum. Mum tried to get Bulimia to move back to her own room, but Bulimia said she was too old to be ordered about. Eventually Mum gave up and picked up the dirty towels in Bulimia's room. Sam refused to sleep in the bed — if he did that it would feel like a permanent move, so he slept on the floor. Feeling very angry and upset, it took him a long time to fall asleep. His other sister Amber thinks it's unfair too, but is just glad Bulimia didn't try to claim her room instead. Sam wishes Bulimia would move out, he feels miserable and there doesn't seem anyone to talk to properly any more. Dad is angry and stays out as much as possible, Mum cries a lot and Amber just goes out, just likes to talk to her friends. No one has time to listen to him any more. Life is very unfair.*

■ *Jane, 19, has won a place at Oxford and is home from University for the summer, the first time since last September. Mum had said that Anorexia was a bit better and Jane had been looking forward to it. Almost as soon as Jane arrived, Anorexia started saying that Mum only loved Jane and didn't do anything for Anorexia. When Jane tried to reassure Anorexia that this wasn't true and point out all the things Mum had done for Anorexia over years, Anorexia started to shout and rage. Jane finally spent the night in a hotel and decided to return to Oxford for the summer. Mum seems helpless, Dad stays away on business and home is not the same any more.*

■ *Peter, 16, is looking forward to spending his birthday money. He's been saving for months for a new skateboard and now he has enough for a really good one. He's arranged to meet some pals at Surf and Skate to choose the right one ... but when he opens his new wallet, he's £20 short. The only person who was in his room since he last checked his money yesterday was Bulimia, he met her at the door coming out. Peter is filled with anger but also with dread – the thought of trying to speak about the money to Bulimia makes his stomach turn over, given the way she has been behaving for months over the slightest thing. Anyway, the money is probably gone by now. Peter decides to take up Jake's suggestion that they share a flat.*

■ *John, 11, has been looking forward to playing the lead in the school play and has been rehearsing for months. Despite knowing about John's excitement and the time he should leave the house, on the night of the performance, Anorexia is in the bathroom and won't come out. Mum and Dad are angry with her, everyone is upset. John can't get showered and ready, and in the end he leaves still wearing his school clothes; his evening seems spoiled.*

(The stories above are all from the EDA helpline. All names have been changed.)

Many people quail before Anorexia's aggression over the least incident, out of all proportion to the perceived provocation. It is frightening to watch someone you know and love, probably have known all her life, behave so out of character. Even Anorexia's face seems distorted. Where others wouldn't react to trivia, Anorexia will show real rage, going right over the top. Having lost track of reality and any sense of proportion, she will shout and scream and stamp and slam doors, rant about how no one loves or understands her, people favour everyone else more, she may threaten awful consequences. At times she goes right over the top about a favourite spoon ... and the rage can last anything from a few minutes to hours on end.

In the face of such behaviour, many people crumble. Most people are afraid that something they say or do may push Anorexia into even more extreme behaviour.

More lives from the helpline:

■ *David and Mo, faced with Bulimia being charged with stealing or shoplifting, arranged to again increase the allowance they had given her since she left home ... only to find that far from being pleased and trying to manage on this amount, Bulimia simply used it up and demanded more. Bulimia is now threatening that if she doesn't get more in her allowance, she will "have to" go out and steal what she needs.*

■ *Roger and Pauline pay for a flat so that Anorexia can be as independent as she wishes, arranging an allowance despite finding it difficult financially themselves. Installed in the flat Anorexia finds it lonely and asks for a mobile phone, then finds that she can't afford the bills. When she asks Roger about paying the bills, he says, "Tough! Don't spend so much on clothes." So she asks Pauline ... who feels sorry for her and agrees to help until Anorexia can get her finances straightened out. Pauline and Roger had a huge row about it when Roger finally found out ... and somehow the finances never seem to get straightened out.*

■ *Grace and John are very distressed when Bulimia is charged with shoplifting again. Last time it happened she promised never to steal again. This time it is reported in the court section of the local paper. A neighbour has also hesitantly told Grace that money vanished from her purse and the only person who had been left in the kitchen where she'd left the purse was Bulimia. John and Grace feel so awful that they are considering moving house. Finally, John agrees to pay the fine again.*

■ *Mike and Betty are devastated when Bulimia is brought home by the police, charged with shoplifting. Bulimia has told them that she has taken food because there is not enough to eat at home and the cupboards are always empty. Mike and Betty are asked to explain the accusation.*

        (The cupboards are indeed bare – but not because no food is provided!)

When incidents like these (all real, but the names have been changed) occur frequently, the stress will inevitably have an effect.

Few parents are equipped to cope with such situations. No matter how much most people want to keep calm, to help and support, human feelings of anger, despair and exhaustion at the sheer unrelenting day-to-day grind of coping will surface.

Brothers and sisters are often very badly affected. As parents struggle to cope with the wildly-swinging moods and behaviour of Anorexia and Bulimia, they are frequently aware of the problems and frustration of their other children – but find it difficult to find ways of giving them time and attention in the face of Anorexia and Bulimia's demands.

Couples find themselves taking different stances and divided about what is happening – they are being fed different stories – and how to respond. Single parents feel their isolation and loneliness even more strongly. And many families, not surprisingly, disintegrate under the strain.

Often it takes a long time for families to realize what is happening – after all, they have probably never met Anorexia or Bulimia before. Relationships have deteriorated to a tangled mess before it is recognized that, in the midst of everything, Anorexia is manipulating, lying and cheating, telling twisted tales – remember, her perceptions are all distorted – then screaming and shouting, blaming everyone else for the trouble.

Few other illnesses or problems take over the family in the way Anorexia does. Few other illnesses bring moral values, such as respect and consideration for others, honesty and truth, into question. The exceptions might be drink or drugs – the addictive behaviours similar in their destructive effects on family and friends. Where chronic illnesses, such as cystic fibrosis, cause stress and exhaustion for the carers, families of Anorexia face the same feelings and have to cope with the additional strain of trying to cope with such a changed personality in their midst – without the support and sympathy.

A few hundred years ago or less, people didn't seem to take the same responsibility for their children's problems. They might have felt sadness, or whole families might not speak to a certain member of the family and show great disapproval, but they did not feel responsible. Out in the community, physical and mental illness were certainly not understood and some may have had a certain stigma attached, but parents were not held to be responsible for a child's problems.

Somehow the idea has grown over decades that It Must Be Someone's Fault and the result is even more misery.

All of which Anorexia is often only too happy to take advantage of, rubbing in Guilt to anyone who will accept it and adding to the despair of her parents. In many families fathers are happy to blame mothers, who seem almost programmed to shoulder guilt in a wide variety of circumstances apart from when eating disorders including anorexia appear.

7

Control issues

Food – only part of the picture

Whatever the causes of the illness – and doctors have been arguing for centuries about all the possibilities – food has now become the focus of all thoughts for Anorexia, blocking out attention to anything else.

However, though food may be the obsession in Anorexia's life, this is only part of the picture.

Parents and other carers often speak of the childlike dependency of Anorexia, who seems to have regressed into childhood patterns – for instance, sitting outside the bathroom door waiting for Mum to emerge; coming into the parents' bed wanting cuddles and comfort; asking at two-minute intervals what she should do. Children are completely egocentric – a baby only gradually learns that the world does not in fact revolve around its own needs. Small children often feel immense frustration at being unable to control their world, which frequently does not make sense to them. With all perceptions distorted, Anorexia retreats into such a world and tries to control whatever she can around her, reacting dramatically to any perceived block to her will. The perceived block may be in the shape of something trivial, such as being given a mug or spoon other than her favourite one; it may be in the shape of a criticism imagined or real or in the shape of a request which to everyone around her seems perfectly reasonable and has been part of the household routine for years. Or the block may be nothing obvious to anyone but Anorexia – a "look in the wrong tone" is enough. Perhaps Anorexia has dwelt on a past situation that has caused annoyance to her but hasn't been noticed by anyone else. And, like a child, Anorexia frequently goes completely over the top in her reactions to the least provocation. She will scream, shout, stamp, bang doors, accuse everyone around her of deliberately annoying her. And threaten suicide.

Locked into extreme fears of the effect on her body if she eats and swallows the least thing; disgusted with her perceived lack of strength over food; terrified by a childlike lack of understanding let alone control of events around her; terrified of being abandoned and alone, Anorexia's world becomes a very dark, hostile place indeed.

Like a child, Anorexia feels dependent on her main carer, but at the same time resents what she perceives to be control over her life; she really sees no choice for herself in her own life. Families, and in particular her main carer, have become people who are trying to thwart Anorexia. For instance, tidying the kitchen after preparing a meal, or clearing your own dishes after eating, long part of the family routine, to Anorexia have become incomprehensible demands designed especially to ignite Anorexia's spectacular temper.

Nobody loves me, everybody hates me

Knowing that a family member is ill, families try èverything they can think of in their efforts to help Anorexia, to prove somehow that they do indeed love her, **something she cannot hear no matter how often or in what way it may be expressed**:

- The family give in to her demands? – *she demands more.*
- They make her favourite meal? – *she refuses to eat even that and accuses them yet again of not understanding, even of telling lies about her weight.*

- They try to avoid annoying her? – *she finds other things to annoy her as well as the original irritation.*
- They do things to please her? – *but nothing is pleasing, nothing is enough.*
- They avoid mentioning the disgusting mess left in the kitchen or bathroom and clean up after Bulimia rather than face another screaming tantrum? – *the messes become more frequent.*
- They avoid mentioning the invasion of their own privacy in the bathroom or bedroom? – *Anorexia simply ignores or is not aware of any silent protests or resistance.*
- They lend Bulimia money? – *she "forgets" to repay it or expresses amazement at their selfishness in mentioning it.*

And each time anyone crosses Anorexia she will shout and scream and threaten dire consequences in her attempts to control all around. The whole illness seems to be about control – overcontrol, lack of control, out of control.

Frequently, a parent will give up work or seek early retirement to try to support Anorexia and Bulimia. Others become so exhausted by trying to cope at work and at home that work suffers and they become ill (see Chapter 16).

Can Anorexia control *you*?

Some family members, ill with worry, have begged and pleaded with Anorexia to eat. Others have tried coercion and threats. All to no avail. Life can become a long war, with daily battles as Anorexia tries to establish control and prove to herself as well as others that she does not need to eat.

Although much of Anorexia's behaviour is childish or childlike, Anorexia also seems to have had a long training in psychology, a first-class degree in manipulation, and can easily identify the people who hate rows and confrontation, those who are so worried by her illness that in relation to Anorexia all family rules are suspended, those who are frequently so exhausted by the whole struggle that they simply give in in the end to whatever demands she makes, she knows she just has to push hard enough, apply enough pressure ...

Standing up to Anorexia is very scary; after all, she has made terrible threats in the past and may even have carried out some of them. If you feel Anorexia has established control over you, what do you think you can do? Do you feel completely helpless, totally overwhelmed and powerless in the face of the aggression? These are very common feelings among all carers.

Perhaps you feel that if only you could find the right approach, you could make Anorexia eat sensibly and then she would get well again? If only ...

Can you – or anyone else – control Anorexia?

Over centuries carers, doctors and nurses have tried to persuade, cajole, threaten Anorexia into eating. In hospital, force-feeding or drip-feeding have been used, as well as denying Anorexia visitors or books or access to radio or TV until she gives in and eats. Anorexia sees all efforts by whatever means as a battle of wills that she will win come hell or high water. When subjected to feeding without choice or consent – even when Anorexia's life has been in danger – as soon as The Treatment is over Anorexia will immediately return to self-starvation and her compulsive drive to be thin. In the past, before the recognition of Anorexia's under-lying emotional problems, sufferers frequently complied under protest with a hospital regime only to return on discharge to their former habits. Anorexia seems to hold all the cards:

> *At the clinic, the doctor says I have to make my daughter eat, not to let her leave the table until she has eaten. I've tried absolutely everything I can think of to do just that, even before she was diagnosed – discussions about health and nutrition, cajoling her, threatening awful consequences if she doesn't eat, even bribery. Some nights we've sat there for hours. Nothing works, but the doctor just won't believe me. I asked if someone could come and show me how to*

make my daughter eat. The doctor said I just wanted to
pass the buck.

(EDA helpline)

The answer therefore to the question is no, you can do nothing to
control Anorexia – you could try arguing with her, tying her to a
chair and forcing food into her mouth, or kneeling on her chest
while someone attempts to get food past her lips, but it is very
unlikely that you will succeed that way in getting her to eat.
Anorexia does indeed hold all the cards and will win every round
by fair means or foul.

**No one can control another person. You can do nothing
to control what Anorexia does or does not, will or will not,
do. But neither can Anorexia control you – unless you allow
it to happen.**

Perhaps, however, you can motivate Anorexia toward the
thought of changing her behaviour?

8

How bad can it get?

How bad can it get? The answer unfortunately is – very very bad, for sufferers who put their lives at serious risk by restricting intake of food, by upsetting the balance of minerals and other essential nutrients for their bodies, and yet who seem to have no real comprehension of the danger they put themselves in. And, of course, for carers who see their much loved son or daughter or partner physically disappearing before their eyes and their personality change dramatically. Few carers happen to have had some useful professional training, in which case they may have some idea of what might help. However, the frustration remains the same, perhaps causing even more difficulties for those carers from the medical and other health professions, who find that all their training gives them no more help in knowing what to do when their own family is affected.

There appear to be different degrees of the illness anorexia nervosa. With help and support, some people recover within months or a year or two, while others struggle for years but "make a recovery", enough to allow them to work and lead a relatively ordinary life. In some cases, Anorexia takes over completely and life for the sufferer, and for her family, becomes a nightmarish struggle over years.

Although there are obvious similarities, every sufferer is individual and Anorexia and Bulimia will behave individually. When carers meet they find much common ground in their feelings – despair, sadness, helplessness, anger, misery – about the difficult behaviour of the sufferer within their family, but there are also differences in the path taken by the illness depending on age, circumstances and situation. To gain more knowledge of the illness see Janet Treasure's excellent and very practical book *Anorexia nervosa: a survival guide for families, friends and sufferers* (1997).

Emphasized throughout her book is the importance of support to the sufferer and the crucial part families can play in assisting the recovery, which is frequently long and slow, with many steps backward as well as forward. Part of the despair of families comes when, having watched the sufferer take several hesitant and painful steps forward, they begin to relax thinking that Anorexia has released her grip and gone on holiday, only to find that suddenly – and often for no recognizable reason – everything changes again. Three steps forward, two back – ten steps forward, several back – is a common pattern:

I thought things were going well. Although my daughter (15 now) was very thin, her weight seemed reasonably steady and she even seemed to be making some progress. We saw the GP several times, my daughter was sent for various tests, she saw a psychiatrist, then as she was "making progress", the doctors discharged her and everything 'official' stopped. Then suddenly a month ago, she cut down drastically on what she would eat and began to lose weight dramatically. Her hair started falling out. Last week we saw the psychiatrist again who told her she must eat. The psychiatrist also told me off and told me it was my duty to make my daughter eat and said to come back in a month ... I've tried sensible talks about our bodies needing energy (she knows them word for word); coercion and threats; bribery; getting angry ... now she says if I mention her eating again, she'll stop drinking too. What do I do?

(Carer, support group)

Luckily, the carer in this case was a nurse and recognized that her daughter's condition was becoming critical. The girl concerned was admitted to hospital two days after seeing the psychiatrist who had simply dismissed the mother's concerns about hair falling out and her daughter's BMI (Body Mass Index, the relationship between height and weight – I had never heard of it until my daughter had been ill for over two years!).

Families who work as a team to support the sufferer are crucial ... but families themselves need help in knowing *how* to help and *how* to cope on the long road to Anorexia's recovery. Most families interact on a daily basis, have their daily ups and downs, big and small disagreements, happy spells and sad ... and have no idea how to cope with behaviour they have never encountered before; to meet it within their own family is devastating.

A few more comments from carers who have phoned the eating disorder telephone helpline:

▪ *I feel so alone. My daughter won't see the doctor, but she's so thin I think she'll break – she says there's no problem but everyone else says she has. I think she has anorexia. What do I do?*

▪ *We are at our wits' end. My daughter has started drinking heavily – she says when she drinks she doesn't eat. Her main goal in life is not to eat. If either of us says anything she screams at us that we just don't understand and to mind our own business.*

▪ *It breaks my heart to hear my friends talking about their children going off and getting on with life. All our children are in their late twenties. The others are all working, some have gone off travelling, some have gone to university and college, some are married and having babies. My daughter lies on the sofa looking at teenage magazines, doesn't go out, doesn't bother any more about her friends. What will happen to her?*

▪ *I've tried so hard to be understanding and not to comment when she's had a binge and there's absolutely nothing in the cupboards. My other children are not so understanding – they're really fed up with M and think I just let her off with everything. Last week I came down in the morning and there was nothing left for breakfast – no cereal, no bread, no eggs, no nothing at all – and I lost my temper with her. She said I didn't care about her, don't love her and would obviously be better off without her. She said she was going to kill herself. Every day I wonder if today's the day when ...*

■ *It drives me mad to have her at my heels all the time. I can't even go to the bathroom – she'll be waiting for me, sitting on the stairs when I come out. She'd come in with me if I didn't lock the door.*

■ *My first husband committed suicide nine years ago and had mental health problems for years, starting when he was a teenager. I remarried five years ago. My daughter didn't know about her father's suicide until two years ago, then she developed anorexia. I'm feeling ill with worry, she's so nasty to me all the time, and it's affecting my relationship with my husband. I'm afraid he'll leave me.*

■ *My daughter is a teacher. She comes home earlier than everyone else and eats everything. Then my sons, 16 and 14, get home and there's nothing to eat. There are endless rows between the three of them and they all blame me. The boys say I make excuses for her, she says I just don't understand. I can't understand, I wish I did. Everything I do is wrong for her.*

■ *I lost my temper and told her to leave if she couldn't accept that other people have rights. She's told everyone in the family that I don't love her and don't want her and want her out. I feel so awful.*

■ *Why is she so horrible to us? We do try to understand, but nothing we do is good enough.*

■ *My daughter has stolen money from me and from her brother, I think for food even though I had done the usual shopping. There was plenty before she binged. Also from two of her friends whose mother phoned me. When I told my daughter about the phone call she said now she knew who were her real friends, as if they had no right to complain. When I told the*

*doctor he said, "Had she been shoplifting too?!" I am deva-
stated, how can I ever trust her again?*

■ *It's about control. Anything she can control, she will, including
us and her friends, in any way she can. This includes shouting,
screaming and threatening to kill herself. She is so nasty sometimes.*

■ *She sort of sets things up to prove that people don't care about
her. The least little thing is taken as proof that she is not
considered, that no one really loves her. Trying to remember
what she decides from day to day is impossible.*

■ *Why is she so angry all the time? At best she's on the edge of
irritation, looking for provocations. At worst it's full-blown
hostility and aggression, all the time. Nothing is right, ever.*

■ *When I asked the doctor what I should be doing, how I could
help, he said he didn't know. He suggested I speak to the
consultant, but when I asked to speak to him, he refused. I
worry so much that I might do the wrong thing without
knowing, and make my daughter worse.*

■ *The whole family is exhausted trying to cope.*

■ *My husband is on the verge of leaving – he says he can't take
any more. He thinks I'm much too soft with her but I know
she's ill and I don't know what to do. It's so awful watching
her, waiting for the next incident.*

■ *It's like a kind of grief, only it goes on for ever, you never get a
day off. When my mother died I was sad but it wasn't like this.
I've lost my daughter, the child I brought up isn't there any
more. The person who is here doesn't like me and I don't know
what I've done. She criticizes everything I do no matter how
hard I try.*

■ *Why can't anyone tell me what I can do to help? Or what not
to do to make things worse?*

■ *I used to do a big shop once a week, now I try not to keep too
much food in the house, even though it's a nuisance having to
spend more time shopping. If my daughter eats everything in-*

tended for the family meals for two days, should I go out and buy more (which I can't really afford) or tell her to replace the food (knowing that she has spent all her money on beauty treatments) or what? If the food is not replaced, then no one eats. Everyone is suffering and I'm worn out.

■ *My daughter can't cope with – hates – people coming to the house. In the past we always had an "open house" for friends who dropped in for coffee and so on, who stayed for meals, who stayed for weekends and holidays. Now, few people visit, partly because my daughter is so unpredictable. She can be really unpleasant, can even be downright rude while they are here and they don't know how to respond.*

■ *Sometimes people have been invited and I then find that there's no food left out of the shopping I did for the meal or coffee or even a biscuit. Not to mention my own embarrassment at her behaviour towards long-standing friends, people she's known for years.*

■ *I wish someone could sit down with me and listen, then tell me if what I'm doing is right, and if it's wrong, what would be better. I think I'm going mad with all the demands at work and at home.*

■ *My doctor says I should "make her stand on her own two feet, make her be independent". If I told her to move out and get her own place, she'd see it as rejection. Anyway, how can you put someone who feels about 10 years old out to fend for themselves?*

■ *Most of her friends no longer see her – I think they find it difficult to cope with her demands and I know she took money from at least one. She feels rejected, but I can understand how her friends feel too.*

■ *I left my husband because of his constant bad temper and awful rages. I wanted to protect my children as well as myself. I've brought my children up on my own. Now my daughter has anorexia, has the same sort of temper and rages – do you think there is a connection? I worry so much that she has the same sort of problems as her father – he has spent his life alienating his family and friends, people just keep away from*

*him. I can't bear the thought of the same happening to my
daughter.*

▨ *When anything annoys her, my daughter just gets in the car
and drives here no matter what time it is. Several times recently
she has arrived in the middle of the night, bursting into our
bedroom and waking the whole family by crashing about and
shouting. Now I can't sleep – I keep waiting for the cars to pass
or to stop at our house. I feel ill with worry and stress.*

▨ *My feelings are all mixed up – I feel so sad to see her, it's
obvious she's ill and desperately unhappy, but I feel angry at
her behaviour too and the way it's destroying our family.*

▨ *My son M came home from hospital three weeks ago. He
started a new job a week ago. How can we help him? We
don't have any contact with the hospital at all now he's home
and we don't know what to do ... we're afraid we'll do the
wrong thing. My younger son is 13 and is refusing to share the
bedroom with his brother again because of all the awful things
that happened before M went into hospital. We're afraid of it
all happening again.*

▨ *My daughter's life was in danger and the doctor decided she
should be in hospital, very much against her wishes. She was
"sectioned" (under the Mental Health Act). Now she hates us,
just hates us, she blames us for sending her away, for rejecting
her. She is eating in hospital, does whatever the staff say – and
says she'll do whatever she has to to get out. Then – she's told
the staff and us too – when she gets out, she's going to stop
eating, and she's "going to get us back for what we've done to
her." Did we do the right thing to agree to her going into
hospital?*

(A postscript to this call – the daughter did exactly what she
said she would – ate while in hospital, complied with
whatever was required of her, then stopped as soon as she
persuaded Authority that there was no reason to hold her
under the Mental Health Act. Once home she set about
starving again; aggression and hostility toward her parents
and siblings became physical. Eventually she agreed to
become a patient again voluntarily.)

Friends and family can support the carers but rarely have a clear idea of what is happening as they too have no experience on which to base any comments. Frequently, friends feel inadequate and helpless, just as much "out of their depth" as the family. Sometimes "friends" simply fade away as the problems go on for years ... adding to the pain and isolation felt by many carers.

Telephone helplines can help families to cope, as can a supportive self-help group where carers can talk to and share with others going through similar problems. Finding a professional who is willing to discuss the problems of living with Anorexia, perhaps through a self-help group, can make a huge difference, or you may be lucky enough to meet a GP or happen to know another doctor/nurse/therapist/social worker with experience of eating disorders willing to help.

9

Can the family survive Anorexia?

So – how have others survived a visit from Anorexia? As with all other tests in extreme circumstances, the answer has to be – with difficulty. As with many other illnesses, there appear to be different degrees of anorexia nervosa, and recovery for the patient may depend on all sorts of factors, including specialist treatment available when needed, financial circumstances, attitudes of doctors, support from friends and family – the existence of or lack of any of these.

However, unlike many other illnesses, coping with a psychological illness is rather different from coping with a physical one as the personality of the sufferer will be affected and the course of the psychological illness will probably be extended over several years. In anorexia nervosa an average length of the illness is about five to seven years although in some cases recovery may be much quicker. In a few cases, especially when specialist treatment is not available, unfortunately the illness becomes chronic. **It is therefore crucial for families not to "burn themselves out" in their efforts to help, or to allow relationships to suffer to such an extent that the family itself disintegrates; if this happens, everyone loses.**

Families must pull together. Easier said than done! This can be said of any family but is especially true of a family with

Anorexia in residence, where the behaviour and demands of the illness may lead to many family disagreements.

Communication is the key to tackling and hopefully finding a way through many of the problems life throws our way, and trying to improve family communication becomes a priority. *Why* has normal communication deteriorated and broken down? As busy family members struggle to cope with the ordinary ups and downs, joys and disappointments of life at work or school, plus organizing meals, sports or social activities and home life, Anorexia seems intent on "divide and rule" in her attempts to control everything around her. By isolating family members from each other, by telling each a different story, "stirring it" endlessly, Anorexia ensures that real communication between them is lost.

Some members simply find ways of being out of the house as much as possible – work, hobbies, social life, all become more and more important to them in the effort to escape what is happening at home. Some members become deeply involved in Anorexia's rituals, believing that the rituals are part of the illness and important to Anorexia and therefore must be tolerated, even supported. Some people become less tolerant and lose their tempers even faster than before. Some become very depressed, seeing their child/partner/friend change out of all recognition with no indication of future improvement. And some become completely overwhelmed by the whole thing and go under. (Looking back I find it frightening to recognize how close I came to complete collapse.) This is particularly the case when there is no one to talk to and people have no idea of the lengths Anorexia, lost in her unhappy and distorted world, will go to get what she thinks she wants. **Don't let it be you! By reading this book and looking for support, you have already made a start to finding information, help and support.**

As accurate information is in short supply, resources thin on the ground – and in some places nonexistent – and specialist help even rarer, it is not surprising that families often need help to "pull together" to support Anorexia in her struggle against the illness.

But some families *have* survived and come out the other side much stronger as a result of Anorexia's visit. This does not happen overnight and, like the course of the illness, often involves two steps forward and one back. No matter how long it takes, as long as the direction is generally forward, it can only benefit Anorexia and your family. Try to think about where you all were six months ago, a year ago and concentrate on any progress made.

In any problem solving, finding a solution or a way through is easier if you can share ideas. So the first step is to get the family around the table and ask everyone, including Anorexia, to outline what they see as the problem or problems. Ask the questions Who, What, Where, When, Why ... Perhaps initially it would be a good idea to stick to discussing one problem at a time. A weekly family meeting? In today's hurrying world, it may not be easy to find a time to suit everyone and compromises regarding activities may have to be accepted in order to find time to hold such meetings. To grow strong enough to beat Anorexia, perhaps Dad may have to agree sometimes to excuse himself from work early, or Brother miss a bit of a session with his mates, or Sister skip an evening class.

Before talking about the problems, setting ground rules is a good idea, such as "Everyone speaks in turn, no interrupting." Again, easier said than done – every family is different and must find its own way – but don't give up at the first hurdle! After all, your family future is at stake. If the first attempt(s) at family discussions end in chaos rather than progress, try again. You may need a more detached friend to help smooth the discussions and keep everyone on track. Long rather than short-term goals are the aim.

When people are living with stress (whether financial, medical, legal, emotional) communication can break down. Any family coping with chronic illness is under considerable strain, and this is particularly true of psychiatric illness where the behaviour of someone who is ill affects the daily life of other family members. No matter how much people love the sufferer, when faced daily with behaviour that is aggressive, manipulative, unpleasant, extreme, that love will be tested to the limit. Therefore anything that might improve matters in the home is worth exploring. **I did – and my explorations led to this book!**

Many programmes have been made and books written on communication. See, for example, Robert Bolton's (1986) *People Skills*, which has sections on submission, aggression and assertiveness, and about resolving conflict ... It may be worth looking in your local library or bookshop for one that seems right for your family. Also worth a look are books for families coping with other psychiatric illnesses that affect many. See, for example, Kim Mueser and Susan Gingerich's (1994) *Coping with Schizophrenia – A Guide for Families* – the illness may take a different course but many of the problems faced by families are similar. (And reading about other people's problems often leads to appreciation of what you *don't* have to cope with!)

It is worth mentioning again the families section of Janet Treasure's (1997) *Anorexia nervosa: a survival guide for families, friends and sufferers*, and Arthur Wassmer's (1990) *Recovering Together – How to Help an Alcoholic without Hurting Yourself* is also very useful too. Written for the families of alcoholics there are many, many similarities in helping the victims of addictions, whose families also find themselves drawn into inadvertently supporting the unwanted behaviour in their efforts to help.

More ideas for survival of families and individuals are given in Chapter 15.

10

You are not alone

Chair

Each day
I give you comfort.
Each day
since we came home together
I support your weight,
increasing with the years.

You should look at me you know,
be aware of the burden I carry,
feel the cracks as my skin rubs, wears.
You should attend my worn springs,
sturdy frame and broad smooth surface.

Why don't you
brush down the worn coat?
Listen to my croaks and groans?
Come here, stroke me, touch
with love the faithful arms
waiting, fearful
that you might not return.

Why don't you
feel the warmth of my heart
beating at the sound of your feet?
Why don't you,
just once,
look at me?

I am tired
of your careless demands,
the way you blindly take
and take and take and take.
One day my inner strengths
                without warning
                      will break.

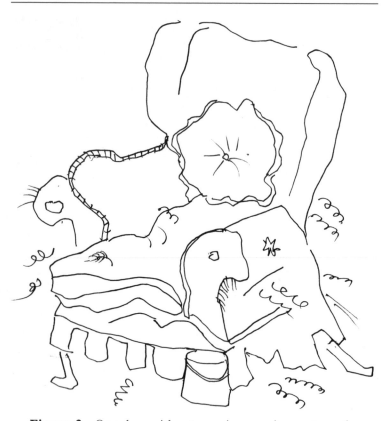

Figure 2 One day, without warning, my inner strengths
will break.

BA (Before Anorexia) life followed its course of ups and downs
involving work, school, family activities, social life, household
organization, in varying degrees depending on age and life stage.
Family relationships too involved ups and downs – as eating disorders frequently start during the teenage years, there are often
older or younger siblings, and with children around squabbles and
rows are frequently part of the day-to-day picture. Every family,
with all the mixed personalities, will have encountered times when
one or two or more people fall out ... In today's world parents
often work incredibly hard to support their families in the best way
possible, putting themselves under great pressure in their efforts

to provide. Families who experience eating disorders in their midst are no exception. Like other families who experience major illness, especially when it lasts for any length of time, relationships and strengths will be tested to the absolute limit; weaknesses will be exposed in glaring technicolor. As one of Anorexia's favourite games is called 'Divide and Rule Wherever Possible', family members begin to experience personal isolation unknown BA . . . .

In any crisis, people feel alone if they feel no one else is going through the same experience. Even in times of great happiness it is sometimes difficult to find the words to share our experiences adequately, but at least in joyful situations our faces and body language can convey what we feel. In our culture over many many years it has been seen as weakness to show our feelings, especially when these feelings are sad and about painful experiences that are difficult to come to terms with, let alone share with others. We have all heard the saying "Laugh and the world laughs with you, cry and you cry alone", and in today's mobile world of scattered families and friends it is even more common for people to feel totally alone when faced with problems.

Many parents talk of having their fears dismissed by professionals, as if it were somehow peculiar to express worry about someone starving themselves, unable to function properly and often literally dying before their eyes, adding to their feelings of isolation and pain.

For anyone who has not shared time with Anorexia during a bad period, it is difficult to imagine the scale of the aggression families may have to face. Even professionals specializing in eating disorders who see Anorexia regularly, find it difficult to imagine this as they only see her in the sheltered, structured environment of hospital or clinic. Even close and sympathetic family and friends can have little idea of the problems unless they have witnessed them, and Anorexia is frequently (but not always) very good at being all sweetness and light when there are visitors.

"Teenage tantrums" is a favourite comment by those who have not experienced Anorexia's rage. Families frequently feel totally helpless, cannot see any way of persuading Anorexia to admit at all that there is a problem – and if they try to enlist help from their GP they frequently find that the doctor knows very little about eating disorders, let alone the best treatments or the need for family support.

Worst of all, parents have probably come across the Blame Factor. Meanwhile, the family itself seems to be falling apart as everyone struggles to cope in their own way, adding to the general misery of all those involved. Unable to find help, let alone support, and frequently even basic information, the isolation felt by families is complete.

In recent years however, thanks to the efforts of individuals who formed the Eating Disorders Association (EDA) – a tiny charity punching well above its weight at the present time! – thanks to the honesty and guts of Princess Diana and others who spoke publicly of their own eating distress, thanks to the greater interest of the press and the public, thanks to the discovery of a genetic factor, thanks to doctors who have realized that families can provide valuable back-up support for their patients, at last things are beginning to change for families – slowly, very slowly, but they are changing.

With the rise of eating disorders in an increasingly-stressed society, more families unfortunately will need help in the future. Anything that can be done to help and support them and anything they can do to support each other will not only help the individual families but also help the deeply unhappy Anorexia and Bulimia in the struggle to understand what must seem a very hostile and incomprehensible world.

It is well worth trying to find the right support for you and the family. You may find it through a good friend or relation, a good GP, nurse or professional counsellor, or through a support group or helpline. EDA will give you a list of what is available in your area, as well as information about the illness, and recommend books that might help; if there is nothing in your area at present, that doesn't mean no one else has experience of anorexia – you might consider starting your own group to find others in the same situation. The longer you struggle, try to cope with the isolation, the more likely both you and the family are to disintegrate.

Wherever, however, you find that support – **remember, the future of your family as well as Anorexia could well depend on it.**

Read all about it!

READ ALL ABOUT IT! THE LATEST THEORY! –
CHILDHOOD? – POISONOUS PARENTS? –
PERSONALITY TRAITS? –
GENETIC RESPONSE TO STRESS? –
NATURE VERSUS NURTURE? –
READ ALL ABOUT IT!

"She was like a Skeleton clad only with skin," wrote Richard
Morton in 1694. Yes, 1694. Because anorexia nervosa has been
given much more media attention over the last part of the 20th
century, it is commonly believed that it is a modern phenomenon.

However, anorexia nervosa as an illness has been around
for centuries, and for centuries doctors have argued about the
best course of action to help patients recover. Treatments have
included:

- forcibly feeding Anorexia while ignoring the emotional aspects
  of the illness (on release, Anorexia usually reverted very
  quickly to her former habits);
- separating patients from their families completely (the family
  members, in their worry and fear for their relative, frequently
  could not agree on the best line to take and Anorexia would

play one off against another to enable her to continue with her
dangerous starvation game);
- hospitalization where Anorexia "earned" privileges, such as a
  visitor, or a book to read, or music, or TV, by agreeing to eat;
- educating the main carers in what was necessary to help
  Anorexia in her own home.

Although in recent years the media have given much more attention to anorexia and bulimia nervosa, and Princess Diana as well as
other well-known personalities have bravely decided to speak of
their own eating distress, most people when faced with a visit from
Anorexia to their own family, with or without Bulimia, find out
how very little they know of the illness.

In total ignorance of the illness – it took me two years to
discover EDA – desperate to know what I could do to help my
daughter and unable to find any information, I searched the local
libraries. I finally found one book: *The Element Guide to Anorexia
and Bulimia,* by Julia Buckroyd. Thankfully, I took it home and sat
down to read – and felt physically ill when I read the statement that
"The low self-esteem that is part of the personality of Anorexia
and Bulimia derives from this source. Their parents wanted them
to be something that they were not and could not be – a person with
fewer emotional needs." In common with other parents who have
sought information and help in the same situation, I have spent
many hours sifting over past events trying to work out what I could
possibly have done – or omitted to do – that could have caused my
daughter's illness. When I could come up with nothing very different from the upbringings of my friends' children, I thought how
blind I must be, that there must be something I was missing.

To read the many statements about families made by some
"therapists" and "specialists" is a good exercise for carers – *in
masochism.* Marilyn Lawrence's (1995) *The Anorexic Experience*
considers some of the harsh judgments passed on families (e.g.,
Peter Lambley's (1983) *How to Survive Anorexia* paints a particularly black portrait) and notes that perhaps these judgments have
to be read in the knowledge that "the families who are seen in
treatment when their daughters or sisters have already become
anorexic are families under almost unbearable stress."

As the same therapists and specialists who made such harsh

judgments also ignored and excluded families from the picture as a deliberate policy, they were able to come to all sorts of conclusions about poisonous/toxic/dangerous parents without ever talking to any. While acknowledging that Anorexia saw a distorted image in the mirror and knowing that starvation impairs reasoning and capacity to think properly, they could not conceive that perhaps they just might be getting a distorted image of Anorexia's family from someone who, no matter what was said or done, could not hear or understand or accept any expressions of love. And that being unable to feel any love around them, living in a bleak unhappy world, that is the picture Anorexia will pass on. In her unhappiness and distress it is difficult, even impossible, for Anorexia to remember happy times, to recall all the talents and abilities of past days or to imagine that these times may come again.

While there are indeed families where a father or uncle or cousin or neighbour has abused someone who then develops an eating disorder (or another mental illness) – Claire Beeken's (1997) *My Body, My Enemy* paints a powerful picture of her experiences of anorexia nervosa following sexual abuse by her grandfather, and she describes her family struggling not only with the shock of learning of the abuse by a trusted family member but also with the very real possibility of the death of a daughter – there are many others where anorexia has developed in a loving family with ordinary ups and downs.

It is interesting to note that until very recently help and support for the families was rarely ever envisaged, let alone offered.

There are many such theories, many such books, which tar all families – and most especially mothers as the main caregiver – with the same simplistic black brush. And if I could find them and read them, so too could friends, family and acquaintances, a few of whom may forget all the beliefs, interests and experiences shared in the past. These few simply do not seem to be around very much any more. Families living with Anorexia frequently talk of their feelings of total isolation:

■ *My friends don't phone any more; I think they are afraid Anorexia will answer the phone and they won't know what to say.*

■ *Some of my friends found reasons why they couldn't accept our invitations, so I gave up inviting people in. It's not surprising really, my daughter was often very rude when people came to the house. I think she felt it took away attention from her.*

■ *How can I phone my friends again? It's the same old story, has been for five years without much change. I'm so tired of it all.*
(EDA helpline)

If someone only happens to read a book that stresses all the negative aspects attributed to parents without any real knowledge of the illness, they might never also discover: that the most successful treatment for anorexia, developed at the Maudsley in London but also used in Germany by Michael Scholz, with greatly reduced death rate and fewer relapses, involves training families to support the work of caring professionals; that many families with an anorexic member show no great differences from other families before the onset of the illness; or that, using the same questionnaire, the main carers of anorexia show much higher rates of stress than the carers of psychotic patients (Treasure et al., 2000).

An outline of research in eating disorders would not be complete without reference to the the 20th century. So, read all about it? **Don't** – unless you are feeling strong enough and prepared for the additional pain of the experience, and bear in mind that these blinkered opinions are just that: opinions.

Interesting as it may be – as well as often painful – to read the various theories and opinions developed in ignorance, of far more practical help in coping with anorexia is to contact the Eating Disorder Association (EDA) and if possible others in the same position to share the load on what will probably be a very long road.

12

Research – past and present

Fascinating outlines of various lines of thinking and research over centuries, since anorexia and more recently bulimia were first recorded, are given in both Janet Treasure's (1997) *Anorexia nervosa: a survival guide for families, friends and sufferers* and Marilyn Lawrence's (1995) *The Anorexic Experience*. The difficulties encountered by carers were recognized and noted. For instance, Pierre Janet, an eminent French psychiatrist in the 1890s–1900s, who outlined the way *a patient seeks a support in one of her parents against the other, she promises wonders if her family are not too exacting, she has recourse to every artifice and every untruth* ... Sound familiar?

Without imagination and creativity, mankind would still be living in caves; sometimes these took place in a flash of brilliance when someone made a connection, more often through a long process of trial and error. Medical research involves painstaking trial and error, and whatever the area – cancer, hip replacements, multiple sclerosis or diarrhoea – many lives will be affected in the process.

Throughout centuries medicine men, doctors and scientists have tried and tested ideas, searching for solutions to common and not so common problems. In some civilizations people worked to share knowledge for the common benefit, in others knowledge was guarded and used for commercial gain. And throughout the centuries, some (not all!) doctors as well as scientists have felt it important to make statements rather than saying it is their opinion or admitting that they were quoting the latest idea rather than proven fact with evidence to back it. Some feel their position of power would be threatened by an admission that what has always happened is that an idea was thought up, a theory has been developed, funding found and research set up, which seems to prove that theory is right – or wrong. Sometimes unfortunately inconvenient evidence has been quietly ignored or even hidden. And if someone has spent years trying to prove that M is right, he is most unlikely to later subscribe to the idea that perhaps after all X was the case. By then, he (almost always he) has spent years teaching and lecturing on M. It is only when more research is undertaken – and more funding found – that M's ideas are finally discredited.

It is notable that it only seems to be in the late 20th century that blame begins to be attached to parents. Before this, doctors seemed to accept that although parents, in their anxiety about their daughter, might not be consistent in their approach (*Now they try to allure the patient by all possible delicacies of the table, they scold her severely, they alternately spoil, beseech, threaten her ...*: (Pierre Janet, 1890), the families in question had the patient's best interests at heart but found it hard, even impossible, to successfully withstand all Anorexia's many games and tricks. John Ryle, as late as 1936, suggested that good results could be obtained at home *if the situation is clearly and fairly explained to the patients and to the parents also.* However:

> *if the programme initiated at home is not proceeding satisfactorily, treatment is better carried out in a nursing home ... Doctor and nurse must obtain early and full control over the patient and from the beginning ensure that the food provided is eaten ... explanation, reassurance, distraction and firm treatment of the starvation are usually adequate and will ensure a steady and parallel improvement in the mental and physical states.*

Most studies of eating disorders in the past suffered from one common factor – they relied on information given by patients in clinics or hospitals and took no interest in any information from outwith the structured and formal setting, although Hilda Bruch, a leading researcher into eating disorders in the late 1960s/1970s, noted the dangers of theories based on hindsight where assumptions based on current problems within the family were made about family relationships *before* the onset of eating problems. It did not seem to occur to most researchers to question the effects on close family and friends of living with someone deliberately starving herself or clearing cupboards of food intended to last a whole family for days.

Daniel Goleman's (1993) *Emotional Intelligence* outlines the many theories advanced to explain eating disorders – fear of sexuality, early onset of puberty, low self-esteem, overly controlling parents. In one very large study quoted in Goleman (1993) more than 900 girls in Minneapolis were tracked for several years, and it was found that by their middle teens there were 61 girls showing serious symptoms of anorexia or bulimia. According to Goleman, *the greater the problem, the more the girls reacted to setbacks, difficulties and minor annoyances with intense negative feelings they could not soothe, and the less awareness of what, exactly, they were feeling.* Goleman also notes that *overly controlling parents were not found to play a prime role in causing eating disorders*, but rather the effects of growing up in a society preoccupied by unnatural thinness as a sign of female beauty were implicated. Goleman also quotes large national studies of American children, based on parents' and teachers' assessments in the mid-1970s and at the end of the 1980s, which show a steady general worsening of emotional functioning in children 7 to 17 and a rise in rates of withdrawal, social problems, anxiety and depressions, attention deficit problems and aggression. This would tie in with my own experience and observations as a teacher in Britain between 1965 and 2003, as well as with the current regular reporting of incidents of road rage, air rage and even trolley rage in a supermarket. Various theories have been put forward for this, including: the possible parts played by dietary changes in the 20th century; rising levels of stress in a very mobile society where family and friends move around much more than in the past and expectations and pressures have been raised by advertising; difficulties in development of emotional functioning due to parental attention being more limited than in past generations.

The development of a general culture of "Someone must be to Blame", with easy short-term answers being sought, has brought its own pressures.

Although there are always exceptions and there are doctors who do listen with compassion and do their very best to help, parents' experience of being ignored and dismissed has happened so often and there are so many instances that can be quoted (and this is only in my own small experience), the "Someone must be to Blame" culture may be seen as almost the norm, not only with parents of Anorexia but also with parents who have expressed other concerns. For instance, as a baby who frequently woke from sleep screaming with my back arched in pain, on being brought to the doctor I was dismissed as a bad-tempered child and my mother told to stop fussing and just ignore my crying – according to the doctor, I was obviously attention seeking. At five I was diagnosed as having a mild case of spina bifida and it was finally recognized that the waking and screaming was a result of severe nerve pain ...

Therefore, in the study of eating disorders along with all other areas of medicine, various theories were developed and later discarded. It was only by testing out a theory of treatment, which sometimes was horrific when exposed to the searching light of hindsight, that wrong theories could be proved wrong, such as force-feeding while ignoring emotional distress and finding that patients simply endured the procedures until released and then went back to anorexic life as before. Many. many harrowing stories are told of patients' experiences in psychiatric wards. Again, patients and/or their carers who protested or tried to question were dismissed.

Small wonder then that the idea that parents are *always* to blame for their children's problems is only slowly being questioned, small wonder that it is taking years for today's research into the role of genes, environmental factors, the working of the circuitry of the brain and emotional intelligence as well as personal life experiences, to finally percolate through to the far reaches of society as well as of medicine.

Small wonder there are so many awful helpline stories.

Today's research

Today's research places a far greater emphasis on *evidence* to back changes in treatment, rather than conjecture and guesswork, than ever before. New technology, such as brain imaging, has opened up new avenues to challenge the ideas of the past, with studies presently going on into the role of damage to parts of the brain crucial to emotional functioning. Questions are now being raised as to whether, in the development of eating disorders in particular individuals and not in others, such damage has occurred during the dramatic biological changes to the brain during puberty or the possibility that there could be a dietary implication, such as vitamin or essential acid deficiency, at an important time of development, perhaps even in the womb, and several recent studies have noted the links between emotional and behavioural changes following damage to key areas of the brain. One question – which can only be answered by further long-term studies – is whether such damage is the consequence of a neurodevelopmental disorder or a result of the illnesses. However, as noted by Janet Treasure (2003), where in the past eating disorders have often been dismissed as *trivial complaints of spoilt princesses who are being stubborn and wilful, it will be difficult to hold to that position in the face of evidence coming from research into brain imaging.*

Much research is ongoing into the role of genes and personability traits in eating disorders (as well as in other disorders and illnesses), the role of metabolism, tendencies to leanness or more comfortable padding in families. Hormonal signals to the brain are under further study in efforts to understand hunger, satiety, diet, attitudes to food and their relationships with mood and behaviour.

Research is now under way into the role of families, genetics and stress as factors in the development of mental illness and their role in recovery. In education, for many years parents found a line drawn at the school door over which they were not encouraged – or were even forbidden – to step. The same attitude so prevalent in the medical profession in the past could also be seen in the teaching profession – "we are the professionals, we know best". Thankfully, in education things have changed, with the crucial role played by parents in helping troubled children recognized. In many areas of health care (e.g., cancer, motor neurone disease, diabetes) carers are now recognized as valuable collaborators in supporting professional efforts and are given care plans to follow, numbers to contact if things go wrong. Had I been right initially in thinking that Jay had cancer, I would have been viewed as a valuable member of a care team.

So why not in mental health? The main reason seems to lie in the fact that many mental illnesses, including anorexia nervosa, may be triggered by stressful life events rather than, or perhaps as well as, physical causes. Reaction to stress is a very individual thing – what acts as a final straw to one person may be inconsequential to another and reactions to major traumas can differ greatly. Because stress is such an individual thing, it is impossible to generalize – but generalizations frequently have been given in the past as stated facts after someone has put forward a theory and time and resources have been put into proving it. With modern methods of research involving more rigour and demands for evidence, as well as new technology, this is changing as previous ideas are being challenged.

Puberty

Puberty has always been recognized as a time of major change and transition, with turbulent feelings and intense reactions the norm as well as the obvious physical development. Some communities mark such changes by, for instance, initiation or religious rites, although in today's mobile world where many families are scattered this seems to be practised less often. It's a time of testing boundaries to the limit, with few progressing smoothly from child to adolescent to adult. Whatever society a person grows up in, however remote or urban, part of growing up and becoming independent is finding out what happens when that testing goes too far, what happens in various circumstances and in new experiences while living at home or away. In animal and bird life, youngsters reluctant to leave the parental home are sometimes given a hefty push. Human parents have been known to sigh with relief when a much-loved but "testing-to-the-limit" young person leaves home to become independent ...

Much research has now been undertaken into the biological changes around puberty that lead to changes in brain and emotional functioning as well as thinking capacities; several such studies are quoted in Daniel Goleman's (1993) *Emotional Intelligence*. Although an eating disorder may begin at any age, the majority make themselves known around puberty. The age of puberty seems to be getting earlier in our society, and younger children also appear to be developing eating disorders – the youngest I know of was eight years old, but I know of at least one clinic that treats children as young as six. *Something goes wrong with maturation at puberty*, said Arthur Crisp at the 2000 Carers' Conference, and today's research is following up on that investigation.

Triggers

It is recognized that some people – the proportion given may vary but is usually described at about one-third – who suffer eating distress have also suffered sexual abuse; in their case the stress of the abuse itself along with the strain caused by keeping such a thing secret – especially if a family member was the abuser and family reactions to the revelation of such behaviour is an added factor – results in eating distress, and food becomes the focus of the sufferer trying to regain control of her life. Claire Beeken (1997) tells such a story in her moving book *My Body, My Enemy*.

That leaves about two-thirds of sufferers who develop an eating disorder because of some other cause. Bereavement or the loss of a friend, great disappointment, moving house and bullying also seem to be triggers, all of which are echoed frequently on the EDA helpline. *Some sufferers have led tragic lives, whereas for others Anorexia Nervosa appears to be the only blot on the landscape* (Janet Treasure, 1997).

In Western society today there is enormous stress placed on individuals by the relentless emphasis on having the Right Look, the Right Clothes, the Right Food (according to industry rather than dieticians) and so on – this too could be a trigger. At a time of great biological changes in the body, this could be a last straw in coping or not for a young person.

When change is a major problem

Research (Prochaska and Di Clemente, 1982; Velicer et al., 1996; Prochaska and Velicer, 1997) has shown that people do not suddenly decide to change their behaviour. Instead, anyone making a major decision – moving job or house, getting married – goes through a process of consideration. Some people, like me, when faced with a major decision, even make lists of pros and cons! The same holds true to an even greater extent for someone who feels their behaviour is contributing to their problems. **First, however, must come recognition and acceptance that at least one aspect of their behaviour could be causing a problem.** And for Anorexia and Bulimia the idea of change seems really difficult to contemplate, let alone the idea of actually following through a plan of action even though it might just save her life.

This difficulty is shared with many others, especially people who have an addiction to a drug or alcohol. Anorexia's behaviour in denial of her problems is equally as vehement as that of an alcoholic or drug addict: it is everyone else who is out of step, she herself is in complete control of the situation . . . If only everyone would stop worrying and just let her get on with her life . . .

Watching someone losing weight to the point of emaciation, seeing someone so weak that climbing stairs becomes a task akin to climbing Mt Everest, knowing that the binge and vomit cycle could result in serious health problems if not death – is emotional agony. And the agony for carers is made much worse by the knowledge that it is self-inflicted. No wonder feelings of helplessness and hopelessness are frequent.

Links?

All these feelings are echoed in the experiences of people who live with anyone addicted to alcohol or drugs. Arthur Wassmer's

(1990) *Recovering Together* outlines the recognizable path that addicts and their families (codependents) go through. Although some of the steps for the addict may be different, for the main carer, whether parent or partner, the path can be strikingly similar to that of families living with someone with anorexia and bulimia nervosa. I followed the path myself all the way down through:

- *Codependent accepts social isolation (not worth the embarrassment).*
- *Terrified by aggression.*
- *Life becomes coping with a series of emergencies.*
- *Codependent hits bottom – at end of rope – chronic depression – gives up on addict/self – may consider or even commit suicide.*
- *Or begin to recover.*

According to Arthur Wassmer, recovery for codependents includes <u>carers</u> seeking help, counselling, support from others in the same position, beginning to focus on self in a healthy way rather than on partner/child. It also includes: *stopping carers from enabling and taking responsibility.* **Only Anorexia and/or Bulimia or the addict can really change things in their own lives. Accepting that is the hardest hurdle.** It is a natural human reaction to want to help your child, to want to help someone who is obviously suffering, whatever it takes. Deciding what it takes is difficult if not impossible in the absence of information or knowledge, let alone help, support or guidance.

Alcoholics, addicts and Anorexia seem to share one common factor – a compulsion to continue their behaviour in the face of all opposition, whether emotional or reasoned, and frequently at the cost of losing work or relationships. Or in Anorexia's case especially, <u>life</u>.

Through the helpline and from talking to carers, I know that other problems often occur in families with anorexic members – autism, Asperger's Syndrome, ADHD (attention deficit hyperactivity disorder), OCD (obsessive compulsive disorder), addictions. For example, many carers may mention that their father and grandfather were alcoholic or may reveal their extreme distress that not only is one of their children autistic or suffering from OCD, coupled with the difficulties they have faced in coping with the problems caused by this, but that now they are also struggling to cope with Anorexia. When I came across Arthur Wassmer's book on *Recovering Together* I literally gasped – and wept – at the similarities of experiences between carers for Anorexia and those of alcoholics and other addicts in meeting aggression and denial. I found the parallels startling.

Current research at the Maudsley, London, by Janet Treasure and in Germany by Michael Scholz shows that training and supporting families in efforts to motivate Anorexia and Bulimia, in addition to individual therapy as appropriate, show much higher rates of success – if rates of success can be measured by reduced death rates and relapses – than other methods. These treatments involving the families seem to echo the most effective treatments developed over many years in such addictions as alcoholism.

Some relatively successful treatments have been developed in many clinics and hospitals but little or no contact is made with the family apart from – perhaps – asking for information about the onset of the illness. From the structured, protected and understanding environs of an enclosed world, sufferers are then sent home to real life, including work and study, family and wider relationships that might or might not be supportive or understanding. Without any support or family guidance as to what to expect or how to help, sufferers are frequently doomed to relapse when stress develops – and what life can be led without stress and change of one kind or another? Life *is* change. Months of work can and frequently does unravel because on discharge families and friends have no idea of how best to help and support the sufferer who, under individual stress, is still prey to the same worries.

In treatment of addictions, alcoholism and other compulsive self-destructive behaviours it has been found that anything that can lead to the sufferer's own motivation to change is an important key. Unless that personal motivation is there, little can be done in the long term, and this can be applied to trying to motivate Anorexia and Bulimia to use that incredible willpower they possess to fight the illnesses rather than their family. (See "How to be a motivational carer" on p. 197 (based on a workshop by Gill Todd) and Chapter 15.)

Recent research (Soren Nielsen et al., 1998) shows that early recognition and intervention can play a significant part in reducing figures that quote tragic rates. The longer the gap between recognition of eating problems and appropriate intervention the more likely the disorder will become chronic or result in early death.

Questions . . .

So, are eating disorders due to:

- a form of addiction?
- an unusual individual reaction to personal stress which may involve, for instance, loss, moving house, bullying, family problems, coming home to find your husband in bed with a 14-year-old?
- an unfortunate combination of genes?
- an extreme form of OCD?
- physical changes in the brain, due perhaps to genetic make-up, perhaps to lack of vitamins or other essential elements in diet at such a crucial developmental time as puberty?
- the result of difficult childhood experiences, possibly again at a crucial developmental time?
- a combination of any or all of these?
- what part if any does today's emphasis on appearance and the relentless stress on thinness have on a generation who are pressured by advertising to eat more but are less active than any previous generation?

Still hotly debated in medical circles, no one really knows for sure.

My own theory? Almost 20 years ago, as part of my work I attended a lecture entitled "Diet and the Troubled Child" given by the Head of Child Psychiatry at Dundee's Ninewells Hospital, who outlined how on admittance to hospital he put patients on what he called a "simple diet" – no additives, no colourings, organic food. Not only did much of the distressing and extreme behaviour change or even disappear, such chronic conditions as migraines, eczema and diarrhoea also changed or disappeared. Adding back various items into the diet meant reappearance of aggression or other extreme symptoms.

Much later I attended another talk, by Professor Philip James who had co-ordinated worldwide research into how diet and genetic factors led to higher or lower incidences of heart disease, stroke and cancer; Scotland has one of the highest incidences of these diseases in the world. Through changes in diet, Finland, who 15 years previously had had similar statistics to Scotland, had dramatically changed the numbers of people dying prematurely from cancer, heart disease and stroke. Professor James spoke of the genetic changes seen in people who had, as part of an experiment, changed their diet from a diet high in fat and sugar, to one with little fat or sugar but lots of vegetables and fruit.

From these two talks I learned that food can and does affect behaviour and genes. In school I witnessed a quiet pupil, whom I had known for two years, have an intense negative reaction after drinking bright-orange diluting juice at a party, changing in minutes from a relaxed child having a snack to running wildly around yelling uncontrollably. He was unable to calm down for some time. Later he was identified as having an allergy to tartrazine, which was eventually banned as a food additive. Similar findings for change in behaviour connected with diet change have been noted in studies of prisoners and levels of violent incidents.

As a consequence of professional experience of over 32 years in nursery and primary education, including: teaching whole families of children in different classes; working with some very troubled children; specialist knowledge of childhood development from 3 years to about 12; a long-time interest in the part played by diet in the development of educational and behavioural problems ... and adding together all the above *plus* years of: living with Anorexia; listening to parents on the helpline; meeting and talking with parents; reading books and research about eating disorders and their development; listening to professionals lecturing and in discussion ... I have reached the conclusion that something in our environment – possibly diet? – triggers changes in stress tolerance and perhaps in brain chemistry or circuitry, for certain individuals who are genetically vulnerable. And there is far more stress in today's society than ever before ...

The resemblance to other addictive behaviours is remarkable ... when an alcoholic is under stress, he or she is tempted to reach for the bottle; when Anorexia and Bulimia experience stress, eating often goes haywire. As all life involves change and stress, it is impossible to avoid. Once the condition – alcoholism, drug addiction, eating distress – develops and becomes chronic, it is a lifetime struggle to achieve control over the addiction. Early specialist intervention – often difficult given the denials of Anorexia and Bulimia! – and motivational therapies would seem to be the best hope of changing the devastating course of the illnesses.

As I have no money to fund research and no medical or scientific training, I await developments with interest – and hope to live long enough to see my ideas proved or disproved!

The studies and books I have quoted in this chapter are those I have come across which seemed relevant. I am sure there are many others unknown to me.

13

Anorexia, Bulimia and self-esteem

Self-esteem is totally destroyed by Anorexia whether accompanied by Bulimia or not

Whatever the state of your daughter's (or son's, or cousin's, or friend's) self-esteem and confidence, whether he or she is outgoing and bouncy (my daughter's nickname was Tigger) or quiet and shy or somewhere in between, their personality will vanish under Anorexia's vicious attentions.

No matter how often friends and family try to reassure and convince sufferers that all past skills and talents have not been lost, that looks are irrelevant to the love they feel, with Anorexia in control the sufferer can't believe any of it.

Janet Treasure (1997) notes that *AN [anorexia nervosa] is not stubbornness or naughtiness that can be stopped with a show of strength or power. It is an all-consuming irresistible force.* Anorexia is described as *a minx who takes over control of the victim.* This is echoed by people who have been through the hell of having a personal visit from Anorexia (it also sparked the idea for this book):

> *Anorexics carry on a self-dialogue; however, the topic of conversation deals exclusively with her worthlessness as a*

human being. The voices attack constantly, convincing her she is most despicable and not fit to be loved or to exist. This is what they say: "You are a pig; you are disgusting; you don't deserve to eat; you must suffer; you fail at everything you do; everyone is better than you; you deserve nothing; you are stupid; you are ugly; everyone laughs at you; your body is sickening; you are gross; you deserve to die; you should never have been born ..."

(Marcia D, a sufferer)

It was like having a voice in my head all the time, it just wouldn't shut up.

(Jay)

Food is the enemy; hunger is shameful; people are trying to make me fat; I take up too much space; tasting is eating; hunger is strength; one bite even means gaining weight; gaining weight means failure; I'm in control, people are jealous; my hips, waist and thighs are huge, I must try harder to lose more weight.

In discussion with people who currently suffer or who have suffered from Anorexia and Bulimia, the voice doesn't appear overnight. It begins as a whisper and progresses to a deafening roar, in the process drowning out the voices of family and friends.

What is self-esteem? Where does our self-esteem come from?

Millions of words have been written about self-esteem – how it develops naturally through interaction with parents and others around us as we grow up, how it can be affected by adverse conditions, the part it plays in how we cope with life situations, how it can be damaged or even destroyed and what helps to rebuild it.

Anthropologists have studied and written about the part it plays in various cultures and societies ancient and modern; psychiatrists and psychologists have developed theories about how people develop self-esteem – or not – and tried to work out ways of building or rebuilding it, and much debate has ensued. Have you looked recently at the sections in libraries and bookshops on self-help, therapies and personal improvement?

Alex Yellowlees' (1997) book *Self-esteem and Eating Disorders* notes that *self-esteem has two fundamental components: self-competence and self worth.*

Self-competence is to do with:

- being able to cope with the basic challenges of life;
- having confidence in our ability to think for ourselves;
- having confidence in our right to attempt to meet our needs, physical and emotional;
- having confidence to assert our rights and achieve our goals.

Self-worth is more to do with our sense of self-respect and the intrinsic value we place on ourselves, involving:

- value;
- significance;
- empowerment;
- basic goodness or virtue;
- being good enough or adequacy;
- entitlement to personal happiness and the enjoyment of the rewards of our efforts.

Now look again at the messages Anorexia is whispering – or shouting!

Our parents and other members of our family

Parents and other family members play a crucial role in the development of self-esteem. Unfortunately, there are some people who are not lucky enough to be given unconditional love and encouragement as they grow up. Some people are belittled and made fun of, unfairly picked on and punished, in some cases even abused emotionally, physically or sexually.

Susan Forward's (1989) book *Toxic Parents: Overcoming Their Legacy and Reclaiming Your Life* puts it like this:

- Our parents plant mental and emotional seeds in us – seeds that grow as we do. In some families these are seeds of love, respect and independence ... In many other cases they are seeds of fear, obligation and guilt. Godlike Parents, Inadequate Parents, The Controllers, the Alcoholics, the Verbal Abusers, the Physical Abusers, the Sexual Abusers and the Family System are the main culprits. Any or all of these could contribute to low self-esteem.

Many people who suffer during childhood from low self-esteem do indeed go on to develop mental health problems; many others move forward as they grow up and outgrow their childhood experiences. However, Susan Forward and others have made the assertion over many years that poor parenting alone predicts mental health problems, including eating disorders; therefore, all parents of people with mental health problems must be abusive in some way.

The same doctors often state: that the parents of people with eating disorders have high standards; that somehow the same high standards have not been applied to their own families and the upbringing of their children; that somehow they have shown no love or respect for their children in their formative years.

In the past, doctors rarely if ever talked to parents, apart from asking, perhaps, for an outline of the history of the illness. In most cases parents were simply ignored and excluded, yet all these assertions were made and accepted as gospel. *Most models (of mental health treatment) viewed the family as a source of "toxins" rather than help* (Mueser and Gingerich, 1994). It is only in very recent times that a few doctors have begun to question what has been assumed for years and what is still assumed by some.

Like most other parents when Anorexia comes to visit, I have spent many painful and fruitless hours going over all aspects and events in my daughter's upbringing. Children learn by example; had I not set a good enough example? When Anorexia accompanied by her pal Bulimia came to visit, she had no scruples about lying, manipulating, taking both money and food meant for others, had no respect for the ideas or lives of others including me. Where had I gone wrong? What could I possibly have done, or not done, to cause such awful mental anguish for my daughter? I had always taken decisions for what I thought was best in the circumstances; I had always tried to encourage my children to do their best and if they did that that was good enough for me; there were house rules based on respect for all of us and sanctions when these were broken; the TV went off while we were eating and we talked about daily happenings. In my daughter's case she often gave a blow-by-blow account of her activities with some scenes acted out graphically; in the case of my son once activities were over why talk about them, why did I want to know?! I *thought* I had done a *reasonable* job ... but perhaps there was something I hadn't seen? Or not been aware of? What had I done, where oh where had I gone wrong?

I went back over the books I had read in the past, both at home and as a teacher, on positive parenting, and could find nothing. I talked to friends about their memories of my daughter, who in my memory lived up to her nickname of Tigger, trying to discover if my own memories of a bouncy outgoing child were faulty. (To my relief they too remembered the Tigger figure, even quoted stories I'd forgotten!)

I quickly became aware of the thoughts and feelings of many doctors, outlined in books and articles, regarding the parents of people with eating disorders. And in common with many many other parents visited by Anorexia, my own self-esteem hit rock bottom.

Finally, five years after my daughter told me about her diagnosis, having lived through spells of soap opera, bad dreams and outright nightmares with Anorexia, I heard about Susan Forward's *Toxic Parents* and went looking for it in the library. I read her descriptions of the behaviour of "Godlike Parents, Inadequate Parents, Controlling Parents" ... had I fitted any of these awful descriptions? I wracked my brains but could come up with nothing. Was I then so blind to my own faults that I did not even recognize them? Many other books give the same message. (These books were written in the last half of the 20th century. Could this be the reason for the seeming sea-change in attitudes to parents and people who develop mental illnesses and disorders?)

Any confidence I'd ever had dissolved and disappeared.

Parents don't need anyone to blame them — they do a good enough job themselves

(Kay Gavan, Maudsley Hospital)

From listening on the helpline, at conferences and at meetings, I would endorse that! Parents' self-esteem is frequently at zero.

Even now, despite all my years of experience, despite everything I now know, when I am tired and low I wonder is there anything I could have/should have seen? Could have/should have done? Or not done? Anything which might have saved my daughter years of suffering?

Friends and relations and teachers

Friends, relations and teachers can have an important effect on self-esteem. Just one good friend who can be trusted always to support you, who loves and cares for you, can repair the damage of life events. A true friend might argue with you but will always have your best interests at heart. That friend might be your gran, might be the same age, older or younger, might even be a teacher who cares, who listens.

But friends, relations and teachers also have the power to hurt and destroy both by verbal or physical deliberate teasing and bullying. Sometimes only a minor remark, at a time when someone is feeling fragile because of other life events, may be enough to cause emotional pain. Just what does a true friend answer when asked "Does my bum look too big?" — a question that has been asked so often it has become a recognized part of many jokes.

Life events

Life events vary from fun and pleasurable to painful and destructive to boring and repetitive and everything in between. If someone meets a series of events that are difficult to deal with emotionally, which can and does happen (remember the old saying about things happening in threes?), hopefully strength of character and good-enough self-esteem will carry them through to a more peaceful time in life.

Two stories come to mind, of Lesley and Peter (both of whom I know personally).

Lesley's story

Lesley was born with a physical disability that caused great self-consciousness as she grew through childhood. Her father was undemonstrative, distant and unavailable, and all through her childhood Lesley strove to please him, to gain his affection, feeling she only really pleased him if her school marks were good. Unfortunately, Lesley wasn't very good at Maths ... He left the family when Lesley was 15. At 17 Lesley went to college in a distant city, still feeling that somehow she must be to blame for her father leaving and for his rare contact with her and her sisters. At 19, Lesley was in the wrong place at the wrong time. She was attacked and raped; the offender was sent to Carstairs, the state mental prison, having been given a sentence that stated "without limit of time". George, her boyfriend of the time, finding it hard to cope with police interviews and with the state Lesley was in, decided to end the relationship. Lesley eventually married only to find that her husband abused her verbally, telling her repeatedly that she was ugly and a slag. Gradually, many of her friends and her siblings left to work abroad ... and her husband told Lesley that she herself must be a reason for them leaving. Confidence and self-esteem very low, years of struggle followed before Lesley recognized that she did not have to accept her husband's treatment of her, that she alone could not make her marriage work. She then went on to pull herself out of that marriage and brought up two children on her own, having gone on to build a good career that gave her much satisfaction. Later in her life, what had started as a hobby in Lesley's life was developed, giving satisfaction and pleasure not only to Lesley but to others too.

Peter's story

A good-looking boy, Peter, had a loving, very "together" and supportive family. Grandparents and uncles and aunts also lived nearby with their families, and Peter had great athletic talent, which was encouraged at home and school. In his teens, Peter's footballing skills were keenly developed and he desperately wanted to be a professional footballer. He was overjoyed to be given a trial for a big team. Although Peter did not pass the trial he was told to try again a year later, in the meantime to keep practising – and watch his weight. He developed anorexia nervosa and spent months in hospital. Since discharge relapse has been a real possibility. He may struggle for the rest of his life with the messages whispered – or shouted – by Anorexia.

Both of these life outlines are real people. Their names have been changed.

But exactly the same experiences might affect another individual in a totally different way. Lesley might have "gone under" emotionally after her father left, might have disintegrated following the physical attack or any one of the blows that life threw at her, and might even have spent her life as a patient. Peter might have gone on practising his football skills until he was accepted as a player by his chosen team or if that was not possible, happily played for another team while developing other skills that might lead to another job.

All experience in life may affect our self-esteem for good or ill, but responses to difficult and miserable experiences that affect self-esteem are very individual, with the same series of events (as described in the preceding paragraphs) affecting others in an entirely different way. In the first example quoted, the events described followed on as if in a devastating pattern – before recovering from one blow, another descended – yet Lesley, with self-esteem battered at times, survived and rebuilt her life without serious mental illness. In the second, Peter found the blow to his

self-esteem, although seemingly on a much smaller scale than that
dealt to Lesley, led to terrible consequences.

The media

Newpapers now have whole sections devoted to guiding our life-
style choices, and specialist magazines are published to ensure we
conform to – or at the very least know of – what the fashion
industry dictates, not only in clothes but also in shoes, in make-
up, hairstyles, furnishings, gardens, holidays ... Not only are we
"encouraged" to be dressed and look according to the dictates of
the fashion and advertising industries but our homes should also
be furnished the "right" way, our bed linen and crockery should
match ... Advertising is *designed* to encourage discontent.

Every society has its own rules and structures, as well as pen-
alties for people who find themselves outside these. Some societies
have developed very rigid class or caste systems, and there are
laws, written or unwritten, in *every* society that impose sanctions
and punishments when laws are broken: imprisonment is one
option; physical and sometimes draconian punishment such as
beating, stoning or cutting off hands are used in some societies;
the death penalty is carried out even in some civilized societies
despite the possibility of wrongful conviction; in some societies
banishment was the worst possible punishment – in savage conditions such as the Arctic or in hunting societies, an outcast would
soon die without the co-operation of family, neighbours and
friends.

However, not all punishments are as openly employed. Much
more subtle pressures can be applied through gossip! And in our
society today pressure is relentless through the media, with magazines and TV programmes offering us constant advice on how we
should look, how our homes should look, offering diets to help us
achieve the "right" look, telling us what we should think and how
we should behave. Adverts now suggest that we are old-fashioned,
if we don't have the latest mobile phone and that we really *must*
move with the times to be taken seriously. And what then, when we
have bought the advertised clothes, our shoes are the right colour,

hair in the latest style, our homes decorated just so? Well, while we were trying so hard to Get it Right, a whole new look has been developed! Individualism is not an option, save for a few who are seen as trend-setters. Politicians today rarely act through conviction and strong codes of ethics; instead, with an eye on the next election when a fickle public may vote them out of power, they operate on simply trying to please the greatest number of voters. Short-term gains frequently win over long-term planning.

From a very early age children are now made aware through advertising of what is acceptable and what they must do and wear to be cool and "with it", the right things to eat (according to the advertisers rather than dieticians and nutritionists). Young babies are dressed in the latest designer styles, and by the time children go to school many are ready to apply pressure to others to wear the same style or risk social isolation. Fashion statements often take no account of children's normal activities, with "fashion" shoes as well as skirts for eight-year-old girls too restrictive to run about, shoes with heels like adults whose feet are fully grown. As these shoes or clothes are usually extremely expensive and last only a short time, many families find great difficulty in funding them while their children remonstrate, *but Mum, everyone has them.*

Poorer children may only have one pair of shoes and one or two sets of clothes, while those with parents who have more money and bend to either trends set by the media or to Pester Power, have a selection of images to show off in different circumstances: for sports – a designer tee-shirt, shorts and specialist trainers can cost a small fortune; for the disco – another outfit; for a dance class ...

Even in school, despite many schools adopting uniform or dress codes, the "right look" is seen as essential – those who don't have it are often subjected to teasing and bullying. Parents who are conscious of the invidious influence of "fashion" and "image" are caught between trying to resist the pressure and knowing that their children may be penalized. Even primary schools find themselves in the position of having to bring in rules about ear-rings, make-up and nail varnish in class.

Body image too has to be acceptable to the perceived fashion of the day. Decoration of the body, by painting, by piercing, by

jewellery, has been part of human society from time imme-
morial, signifying status perhaps, or preparation for marriage,
or war, or hunting. Binding the breasts or waist to alter the
shape of women might have been employed in the past, but it
is only in very recent times that it has been possible for people to
actually change their features, if they are dissatisfied with their
nose or jaw shape, or to change their body shape by plastic
surgery. Whereas in some societies older people were respected
and even venerated for their perceived experience, knowledge
and wisdom, in today's society signs of ageing are disguised,
often in sheer desperation, through hair dye, boob jobs, face
lifts and tummy tucks.

In the past children played with dolls made of wood, of clay, of
rolled cloth, of straw, whatever materials could be used to make a
recognizable baby or small person. Later, they were manufactured
in greater numbers and had china faces and cloth bodies. They
were loved and looked after until they were outgrown. Today,
Barbie and Sindy dolls, made in the image of an "acceptable"
teenage girl, appear with a collection of the "right" clothes for
such specific activities as horse-riding or ski-ing. The message is
once again absorbed: it is necessary to dress the "right way", have
your hair the "right colour" and in the "right style", but above all
to have the "right image".

Magazines are now published for pre-teens to guide them
toward the acceptable image, to give them advice about make-up
specially for their age-group and about how to attract the opposite
sex. Not yet interested in the opposite sex? Oh dear . . .

And in every magazine, newspaper, advert, the faces are bright
and smiling, the bodies slim and toned. And again that message –
this is the way you must be, it is simply not acceptable to be out of
tune with the given image. No mention is made of the fact that
many of the photographs are airbrushed to enhance "the right
look!" Lack of exercise combined with long hours in front of
TV, computer and video, are also major contributing factors to
people being unhappy with their body image. Is it any wonder
that a huge number of primary school age children are already
on diets, unhappy with their body image? Even some girls as
young as seven are beginning to worry about body image and are
conscious of dieting as a way of changing it.

Dieting is often the first step to anorexia and bulimia ... Is it a coincidence that anorexia and bulimia affect the lives of younger and younger people? ... The youngest sufferer I know of is eight years old and I understand that at least one clinic in London has treated children as young as six. ·

For some people a diet may be undertaken before a special event, or perhaps after pregnancy or for health reasons, but for huge numbers of people diets are a way of life today – just look at the number of diet advice books on the shelves, articles in magazines, clubs in existence. Only a small number of people, however, develop anorexia, although bulimia affects a much higher percentage and because of its secretive nature statistics are very uncertain.

The vast majority of parents are loving and caring and want the best for their children, but sadly there are obviously some parents who do abuse their children in various ways. Among the many children I have worked with, I taught: a boy whose father stubbed cigarettes out on the boy's shoulders and arms; a girl who was not allowed to take her tights off for PE because of the bruising on her legs; a girl who was kept in a cupboard for the first four years of her sad life because she was illegitimate. These are only a few within my own personal experience – there are other harrowing stories quoted daily in the media.

The abuse may be physical or emotional, deliberate or unknowing and completely unintentional. For instance, when a child is born to totally undemonstrative parents, the child may imagine that she is unloved (as Lesley did). Only in later years did she come to realize that her father, seen as unloving, detached and distant, simply had no skills in demonstrating affection or love – because he had been brought up in a very reserved, undemonstrative family.

Melanie Fennell's (1999) excellent book *Overcoming Low Self-esteem* also explores in depth the part played by childhood and adolescent experiences in forming self-image and self-esteem:

> ... *although low self-esteem is often rooted in early experiences, it is important to realise that this is not necessarily the case. Even very confident people, with strong favourable views of themselves, can have their self-esteem undermined*

by things that happen later in life, if these are sufficiently powerful and lasting. Examples include workplace bullying, being trapped in an abusive marriage, being ground down by a long period of relentless stress or material hardship and exposure to traumatic events.

I would contend that genetic make-up also plays a part, with people reacting in different ways to stress, some being more prone to different, stressful life events, destroying self-esteem and causing severe and/or chronic mental or physical illness than others. Daniel Goleman's (1993) *Emotional Intelligence* outlines much research over many years that points to the crucial roles the amygdala, the neocortex and the thalamus – all parts of brain-wiring circuits – play in emotional functioning regarding other people and life events. People who can empathize with the feelings of others are at a huge advantage, while those lacking empathy cannot anticipate or understand the reactions of others. Goleman points out that individual make-up in these areas contributes to how an individual copes with stress. If something affects the development or functioning of these areas, surely personality change will result?

Anorexia nervosa *may* develop after horrific experiences within the sufferer's own family. There are also anorexia nervosa victims who:

- have met with awful teachers who destroy confidence in many of their pupils;
- who have lost close relationships through death or divorce or moving house;
- who have been bullied at school;
- who have had dreadful treatment in an abusive relationship or through crime.

I know because I have talked to them. But there are many others with unremarkable backgrounds, much loved by their families, who:

- are visited by Anorexia when they leave home for the first time to study or to work;
- who, like Peter, receive a setback to their future plans or dreams;

- who lose a beloved person through death;
- who are unhappy at the departure of a much-loved friend and constant companion.

There are victims who are remembered as quiet and shy, lacking in confidence; there are others remembered as outgoing and fun with a great sense of humour. The triggers for anorexia and bulimia seem to be as many and various as the individuals involved.

The one thing in common for all people with anorexia and bulimia is a total lack of self-esteem.

Part II

Don't curse the darkness – light a candle.

Unknown

14

Anxious Annie, Soft Sue or Hard-hearted Hannah – the parents' dilemma

For most of life's problems there seem to be guidelines of some sort or another, written by people who have had experience of similar dilemmas. For the parents or other carers of Anorexia there are no guidelines to be found to help with decisions that arise daily, even hourly and often turn out to be life-changing:

- Do you comment or not when you know that bingeing and vomiting or use of laxatives are dangerous activities that can have life-threatening consequences?
- Do you comment or not about what is on someone's plate?
- Do you mention or not the arrival of yet another bill as a result of old drains being blocked by huge amounts of toilet paper?
- Do you acknowledge or not the food missing following yet another binge which means that other family members went to work/school hungry?
- Do you talk or not about your invitation for a special meal you'd planned and had invited friends to share – only to find the ingredients have vanished?

Should you broach these subjects or not, and if so when and at what risk either way?

Mentioning the problems faced by the family because of the sufferer's behaviour, no matter how difficult life is for family members, risks the rage of the sufferer and the possibility of yet another angry and exhausting scene and even the possibility of a suicide threat, which may or may not be serious. Not mentioning these problems might be seen as condoning the behaviour and encouraging continuation.

A further problem is that at different stages of the illness different reactions will be met – to mention the problem at one stage might push the sufferer further into denial and/or depression and possible suicide, while at another stage exactly the same comment or attempt at discussion might be exactly the right thing to encourage the sufferer to seek professional help, to try to control the behaviour for the sake of the family as well as her own sake.

Only the carer can decide, and each decision must be made taking into account factors such as mood and possible reactions and how you will deal with them. Each decision should be taken on the basis of rational thought and judgment – and when you live with a volcano this is a little difficult ...

When faced with a decision, your own feelings and mood must be taken into account as well as Anorexia's or Bulimia's. What will you do if you meet with an adverse reaction? Do you feel strong enough to risk an adverse reaction, yet another scene? Consider whether Anxious Annie, Soft Sue or Hard-hearted Hannah is ready to confront Anorexia, or is it better to ignore it for the time being because there are other more pressing problems needing attention?

When you feel that you really must say something (e.g., about the lack of food left for other family members), preparation for what you want to say can be very important – but not always possible. Perhaps you, or other family members, have commented at the time of discovery and there has been a big row with everyone shouting and still feeling that they haven't really been heard; this seems to be a very common problem for Anorexia's house. Bulimia's family feel aggrieved by the complete lack of consideration in eating all the food intended for the whole family, while Bulimia feels no one understands the compulsion and the feelings following a binge, which may include despair that she gave in to her craving for food, satisfaction that she got rid of it, misery and feelings of disgust, all mixed up together.

Sometimes family members find it is simply not possible to stop themselves saying hard words about Anorexia's or Bulimia's lack of respect and consideration for other people, and sometimes Anorexia and Bulimia need to know just how upset and angry their behaviour makes people feel. Sometimes a row can achieve what months of tiptoeing around a problem hasn't. Sometimes. Decisions again . . .

It is what happens afterward that matters. If the row is then ignored and all the bitter feelings remain, if more food is bought and nothing is then said until it happens all over again . . . and again . . . and again, a very unhealthy pattern is set, every bit as unhealthy as the cycle of bingeing or starvation. A pattern of trying to ignore problems, of trying to pretend that normal life includes bizarre eating problems and rituals.

Anxious Annie is constantly preoccupied about the effect of unhealthy eating – or not eating, or bingeing and vomiting – on Anorexia's health and of doing the wrong thing. Soft Sue wants to help and feels that as it's obvious Anorexia and Bulimia are ill, perhaps their behaviour simply has to be accepted; after all, if Anorexia and Bulimia are ill, maybe they just can't help the distorted thinking, the volcanic temper eruptions, the antisocial behaviour. Hard-hearted Hannah gets really angry and upset about the rudeness, the lack of respect – after all, this wasn't the way Anorexia was brought up. All of them, Soft Sue, Anxious Annie and Hard-hearted Hannah, feel helpless and fearful of doing the wrong thing. All of them spend hours trying to work out what to do, all of them desperately try to find what is the right thing to do to help Anorexia and Bulimia. Many sleepless nights lead to even more stress and exhaustion.

There is no "right thing" to do, no one answer in any particular circumstance or situation met with Anorexia or Bulimia. This is the hardest thing Hard-hearted Hannah and her sisters face. Carers have to remember – when Anorexia, with or without Bulimia, moves in, she is not reasonable, does not feel rational, cannot be logical. It is not possible to reason with the unreasonable, but what is possible is to state what you feel, what you want and your

**reasons for wanting that, while stressing that you still love
your daughter, but really don't like Anorexia's behaviour.**

One day Hannah and her sisters get up after yet another
sleepless night, to find that yet again Bulimia has cleared the cupboards. For once, Annie's worries about making things worse are
swept aside and Sue's objections – that, after all, Bulimia is very
obviously ill and because of this maybe such behaviour has to be
endured – are ignored. Hard-hearted Hannah has taken charge.
She is very very angry – spitting mad! – that no food is left for
breakfast, not a crumb of anything edible, no milk, no sugar, no
coffee. Bulimia has been bingeing during the night and she has
gone out to work without a thought for anyone else in the household (yes, often she's still managing to work, much to her doctor's
amazement; her iron will demands that she continues working
until she gets to the stage of collapse).

Something in Hannah's heart has cracked and suddenly she is
absolutely furious. Really really *really* angry. To get anything to
eat herself Hannah must dress and go to the nearest shop (luckily
only 5 or 10 minutes away, but it might have been miles away).

All day she nurses her wrath, and when Bulimia comes in
Hannah puts into strong words exactly what she has been
feeling. In the past, Annie's anxiety about saying or doing the
wrong thing and Sue's sympathy for the sufferings of Anorexia
and Bulimia prevented such expressions of their own feelings.
But today Hannah has decided that she cannot let this behaviour
pass without comment. She wouldn't accept it from anyone else . . .
And she has had the whole day to rehearse exactly what she wants
to say, so that the words are there when she wants them. Words
about respect for others, words about trying to take responsibility
for behaviour, words about the consequences of the bingeing behaviour. Not the physical consequences for Anorexia and Bulimia
herself – these have been mentioned many times by this stage and
Anorexia and Bulimia can recite them without a thought – but the
consequences of Hannah getting to the end of her tether and the
distinct possibility that people who have lived with Anorexia and
Bulimia for many years may no longer want to do so and put up
with mess in the bathroom, lack of consideration (i.e., no food left
for breakfast, again), rudeness and manipulation.

That day Hannah finds the strength to resist losing her temper with Bulimia, to stop herself retaliating against Anorexia's immediate reaction of rudeness and bad temper, to Anorexia saying things like you don't love me, you can't love me, you don't care or you don't do anything for me. That day Hannah says what she wants to say and then excuses herself saying, *Now, I've said what I want to say, and I want you to think about what I've said and what you Anorexia and you Bulimia can do to improve matters in this house because I don't want the same thing to happen ever again. I love you very much, I always have, but I am not prepared to accept such a complete lack of consideration for other people including me. Now I'm going to listen to some music.* And then Hannah does exactly what she says she's going to do – goes to another room, shuts the door and listens to music. For once, Anorexia is not invited to join her.

It was very clear that a limit had been reached. **And something had to change.**

Later on, Hannah said again to Anorexia:

> *I love you very much, but I meant what I said. I have had enough of your anorexic behaviour and I am not prepared to accept it any more. I hope you will think about what I have said.*

Hannah then put her arms around Anorexia and held her:

> *I love you so much, I can't bear to see you suffer. I want to see you well and happy again. It's because I care that I talk about these things, not because I don't care. If I didn't care about you, I would just let you do what you want, starve yourself or binge yourself to death. I love you and I do care.*

And for the first time since she moved in, Anorexia said she was sorry. And things did change – there was always something left for breakfast for others in the house from then on. Sometimes not very much, but something.

This is a true incident. It happened in my house.

Looking back I can see elements of Soft Sue and Anxious Annie in my own behaviour and the thinking behind it, when Anorexia moved in. And later on the beneficial effects when Hard-hearted Hannah surfaced. Perhaps you

Figure 3 *I don't like Anorexia's behaviour but I love you
very much. I love you so much, that's why I worry about you.
I only want the best for you ... I love you.*

**recognize the three portraits too and how Anorexia and
Bulimia respond to each?**

No matter how difficult it seems, finding the proper time to
discuss matters is important, I believe Hard-hearted Hannah
must find ways of discussing other people's rights in the face of
Anorexia's completely selfish way of controlling the house and
everything around her. Trying to withstand Anorexia's vicious
temper and savage words in her attempts to control is extremely
difficult – Anorexia would try the patience of a saint (all the carers
I've spoken to are very human, including me!). Soft Sue and
Anxious Annie will understandably be very reluctant to stand
firm, and even Hard-hearted Hannah will take what action she
feels is necessary with a fast beating heart and probably a sick
feeling in her stomach. But if Anorexia is to overcome her destructive behaviour, she needs to think about her behaviour and its
effects on others – and if no one ever points out those effects,
Anorexia will conveniently ignore them; that is, if she ever realizes
them.

**But only you, the carer, can decide when the time is
right to tackle an issue and which issue you want to tackle**

at any particular time. If Anorexia is really out of control – or rather in complete control of events around her? – you may have to decide to concentrate on one particular issue at a time; it's not possible to climb more than one mountain at a time. If possible try to find a calm time for discussion – sitting around at weekends, out for a walk, whenever. Make huge efforts to keep your voice calm and nonaccusing, no matter what provocation Anorexia throws at you. Despite Anorexia's attempts to side-track you, try to stick to what you want to say, say it, then ask her to think about what you have said – and leave. Have another activity lined up – and go and do it. You could say:

> *I've said what I want to say and I've listened to what you want to say. I don't think there is any point in saying it all over again, you know how I feel and I know how you feel. Now I am going to go and ... I'll see you later when we can talk again if you want to.*

Repetitions of the same conversation, or variations of it, may be necessary many times before Anorexia accepts that you really do mean it. Standing firm and being consistent when you are feeling exhausted and dispirited is not easy. Often it's like being caught in an ever-repeating loop.

But if your daughter is ever to escape the clutches of Anorexia she desperately needs your help. Perhaps you can find a time when you can say, *I'd like to talk about something I think is important. Is this a good time for you?* If not, ask Anorexia to suggest a good time and be prepared to talk at whatever time that is. Perhaps a whole family conference could be called. Perhaps regular family conferences may be started, with agreed rules such as one person speaking at a time, even with a list of things for discussion drawn up beforehand. If things tend to get fraught and frazzled – quite likely! – perhaps someone might even act as "referee"? There are all sorts of ways to open up lines of communication – each family must find its own way. But the main carer is the one who holds everything together and feels the heaviest weight of coping with Anorexia.

And what do you do if you fail first time round? If Anorexia succeeds in drawing you into a fruitless argument about how much you do care, you can't resist trying to defend yourself against accusations of lack of love or understanding and you end up abandoning all your good intentions of keeping calm? Do you simply give up and forget about tackling the difficult issues affecting your household and let Anorexia have her own way? After all, it's much easier in the short term. But then you feel even more helpless and miserable and inadequate.

You may need help – look for it. There are many books (see "Recommended reading" on p. 203 for a few suggestions), talk to friends who may have experience in dealing with difficult situations at work and have professional training in keeping cool. You may consider finding a class in assertiveness. Your doctor may be able to recommend a counsellor to help, you may find a support group, or a telephone helpline (see "Useful addresses, phone numbers and websites" on p. 201). Try to find the help you need – you may not have to go it alone after all.

Don't give up. Make even more thorough preparations, rehearse with a friend or in the mirror. Practise deep breathing. And try again. The long-term benefits for your daughter, of seeing her loosening Anorexia's tentacles, are what you are aiming for. **If you give up, Anorexia has won.**

The main message is . . .

I love you very much, but love does not necessarily accept all behaviour. I love you very much and want to see you well. You may not like what I am saying at the moment, but I only want the best for you and that is why I am saying this. I love you.

15

Tips, techniques and strategies

Over the years every family will have faced many problems – organizational, financial, health, emotional. Every individual, and every family, deals with these problems, whatever they are, in his or her own way. Some people don't take time to examine and think about a problem, but try to grab it by the throat and shake it, *I'm in charge, do what I say!* Unfortunately, by not looking at all the facts or trying to find helpful information, not only does the problem frequently grow worse but the basic attitude annoys others who might otherwise try to help find solutions. Some people try to deal with problems by avoiding them, imagining that if they don't acknowledge the problem, maybe it'll go away. Again, unfortunately, problems rarely go away, but have a nasty habit of growing rather than going anywhere. Others think *Well, if I can't do anything about it, why bother even trying?* And still others talk endlessly about the problem and all its aspects without looking for possible positive action that might address it.

I believe it is better to try to find some way of coping with or changing either the problem (say, a reduced amount of money to live on) or maybe even change myself ... Can I live with the problem? If not, is there anything I *might* be able to change to make a difference? Possibly shop in different places, avoid temptation by finding different pursuits, or visiting only shops for absolute essentials? Find other ways of bringing in money? Part-time work, retraining? Apply the motto "Do I want it, do I need it, can I live without it?" – and depending on the answers decide whether I can have it ... At least if all the possible options have been considered, the problem has been discussed with others and I've actively looked for a solution, I feel I've *tried my best*, much better than simply allowing the problem to overwhelm me from the beginning. And I've found that the sooner the problem is recognized and addressed the better. By putting off addressing past problems, or giving up too easily, I think I've sometimes made further problems for myself – to add to the existing ones!

To be effective in tackling a problem, it's important first to look at the problem carefully from all angles, consider everything and everyone this problem affects. Some problems are much more difficult than others, but in very old words that still have relevance "two heads are better than one". Look for information wherever possible ... ask the family what they think – have they noticed/experienced the same problem, what do they think might be done to change things? If possible call a household conference to get all views. Ask friends – sometimes they can see things more clearly because they are not directly involved, may have contacts or information you didn't know about, may think of some practical steps you might take to find support or change things for the better. Are there any books about the problem? Any helplines/charities?

In 2000, the Eating Disorders Association (EDA) organized the first-ever Carers Conference in London, where carers from all over the UK were offered talks and workshops to discuss the latest research, new ideas, issues relating to families and a chance to meet other carers and professionals. The question and answer session was a revelation, led by three prominent authorities: Arthur Crisp, Janet Treasure and Bob Palmer. During that session, queries on eating disorders and related physical and emotional aspects were tackled; several times one or other of the speakers was seen to hesitate and gulp, but all questions were answered fully and in depth, honestly and openly. For many carers including me it was their first opportunity to share the experience of such experts.

Along with many others, that day was a turning point. I hadn't realized how much of a battering my own self-esteem had taken, how much my confidence had been shredded, until after hearing the speakers that day, feeling the hope in many of the messages despite hearing some harrowing stories. I began to feel better. I have no words to describe my relief to hear that what was being recommended was roughly what, by guesswork, a lot of trial and error – many errors! – and some sort of intuition, I had been doing. It could so easily have been otherwise. Six months later I realized that I wasn't going to find the book I kept looking for, a practical supportive book by a carer – so I decided to try and write one.

At one point in the Conference the tables were turned, and the professionals asked the question – *What do carers find most difficult to cope with?*

The following were given as among the most difficult aspects for families in coping with anorexia nervosa:

- coping with feelings of powerlessness, hopelessness and guilt;
- coping with sufferers' hostility, anger and rejection;
- coping with lack of logic and unpredictable behaviour;
- coping with deceit and denial of problems;
- coping with how the illness takes over the family and how to keep family life going for other members; and
- coping with feelings of sadness and loss.

All of which I could identify with.

Lack of help, support or even basic information were given as major factors adding to the fear of inadvertently making things worse. Given that all aspects of family life are affected when Anorexia, often accompanied by Bulimia, makes a bid for power and control – mealtimes, food, money, social life, sleep, work, trust – it is little wonder that families frequently feel overwhelmed.

That day I discovered and bought Janet Treasure's (1997) *Anorexia nervosa: a survival guide for families, friends and sufferers,* where I found much of the information I had sought over the preceding years. All books by professionals, however, have one major drawback – professionals work within or from clinics and hospitals, see patients only within that environment, and they go home at the end of a day, hopefully to loving support. As out-patients, Anorexia and Bulimia may be seen only infrequently; as inpatients, they are within a very protective world, removed from the real world. In such a sheltered, structured environment, many rules and sanctions may be enforced that are impossible to follow at home. For instance, many professionals – see Dee Dawson's (2001) *Anorexia and Bulimia: A Parents' Guide to Recognising Eating Disorders and Taking Control* – have stated that families <u>must make</u> the sufferer eat. *What*, they say, *is the problem? After all*, they argue, *that's exactly what is done in their clinics, why not do the same at home? It's only common sense.* Well, yes. Unfortunately, Anorexia doesn't see it quite like that. When glued to a seat by her family who are determined to carry out instructions, Anorexia may simply sit there. No matter how much persuasion is employed, no matter what threats, no matter what rewards are promised, the last thing Anorexia is going to do is eat. She'll sit there all night, night after night, if necessary. Short of tying her up, forcing her head back and her mouth open then pouring food into it, there is nothing a family can do. Even if they could get the food past her lips they'd have to hold her nose to force her to swallow … And if things get really difficult, Anorexia has been known to employ her next trick … not only won't she eat, she stops drinking. All of which adds greatly to family distress and to the general feeling of failure.

Bulimia doesn't see it like that either. She will make all sorts of promises but not change her behaviour one iota. She'll eat a full healthy meal in front of her family, then get rid of it. In hospital, toilet doors can be locked after meals; at home with other people in the household, it is rarely possible to do this. Perhaps the family conspire to make sure there is no access to the bathroom for Bulimia after meals, only to find that Bulimia simply uses towels or sheets. And again, short of physically tying Bulimia up, families are helpless.

It is only later with hindsight, after a daughter or son has recovered, that carers may realize that a particular strategy or technique really helped. The following strategies and techniques are merely suggestions which, with that famous hindsight, I found helped – you will probably find others of your own that work in your own situation.

I must stress that as every case is different, so are the effective strategies that may work at any given time – what worked in my house, for my daughter and me, might not be successful in your own. But it's worth trying, it's worth

looking for anything that might help your daughter. Anything is better than being paralysed by helplessness and
hopelessness. Don't give up, don't let Anorexia and
Bulimia win the first and every other round – keep going.

If things are very bad, it may be necessary to decide which is
the most important behaviour to tackle and to try and ignore lesser
behaviours that can be tackled at a later date. With the two steps
forward, one back, five steps forward, three back, one step forward,
two back, pattern of the illness, there is no one way that will be
right for all situations and at all times. Carers really do have to
"play it by ear", which can be extremely stressful in itself, as there
is no way of knowing until much later what will be helpful or not –
different strategies will be needed at different stages of the illness.
Carers' energy levels may fluctuate too. And if you feel you have
made a mistake, remember that **everyone does and you can
only do your best**. Accept that perhaps it wasn't the right thing
at the right time and move on. Try again. However, having said
that, you may find that something you thought of at the time as a
terrible mistake in fact turned out to be a blessing in heavy
disguise.

With heaps of effort, pounds of love and perhaps a pinch or
two of luck it is possible to reach the day when Anorexia releases
her stranglehold and moves out. Try to find others coping with the
same or similar problems (EDA can give you contacts), or even
better talk to someone who has recovered from Anorexia ... Yes,
they do indeed exist and are out there getting on with their lives.

Practical matters

In the absence of any guidance, I had to make many decisions
about what to do when Anorexia and Bulimia appeared in my
home. With hindsight, the following are the decisions I think
were helpful and which you may like to try in your own situation:

- *To allow everyone to serve themselves.* I would not allow
  Bulimia to pile other family members' plates so high with
  food so that she could disguise her own. I introduced this

new rule for two reasons: to stop Bulimia piling food on my plate and to avoid her feeling her efforts had been rejected if everything on my plate wasn't eaten. Also, I realized that Bulimia and Anorexia had lost any idea of what was a realistic amount to eat in one meal. For some time I insisted on taking over all the cooking again.

- *To make no comment about what goes on to anyone's plate* (not easy) no matter how much, how little, how bizarre, how disgusting, how amazing. Making comments, whether they were meant as encouragement or condemnation or disgust, simply caused more bad feeling.

- *To continue our lifelong practice of eating together at the table, despite more than one suggestion from Anorexia of separate eating times.* My reason? I like sitting round a table talking over the day's happenings. Sometimes Anorexia withdraws completely from eating with others. If this happens, Anorexia's meals will be outwith your sight and you won't know what she is or isn't eating anyway. So, if Anorexia does eat with you try to keep mealtimes as relaxed as possible.

- *To tell anyone who is there for a meal of the eating problems and ask them to avoid mentioning any topic connected with food.* No good my making such efforts only to have another family member blurt out some awful comment that could set Anorexia back months.

- *To buy food on a daily basis only.*

- *To reorganize my kitchen storage – by using glass containers for basics, which show exactly what is inside (or what is missing and needs to be replaced).*

- *When eating, to try and keep my eyes averted from Anorexia's plate.* Any comment, even "a look in the wrong tone of voice" was counterproductive – Anorexia still didn't eat, it only caused a row and bad feeling.

- *To try and keep the conversation general, to think of topics in advance if necessary.*

- *To say nothing if I suspected Bulimia had again lost the battle to retain her food.* To say anything didn't prevent a visit to the bathroom, it only made for bad feeling. This was the decision I found hardest to keep to.

- *At the end of the meal, to try and keep Bulimia at the table,* to keep her talking, anything to distract her from going immediately to the bathroom to get rid of what she has eaten. Depending on Bulimia's mood, it is possible that a discussion of interesting topics may indeed help prevent or at least delay a visit to the bathroom.

It is only now, with that famous hindsight added to a lot of reading and attending meetings and conferences, that I believe that my decisions during those dark days were right and played a part in Jay's recovery, despite her reluctance to accept professional treatment. I have heard of other sufferers who have recovered with little "official" treatment – and I suspect that their families too probably made similar decisions.

Self-starvation

Starvation is really distressing for any human to witness, even more so when it seems self-inflicted, by Anorexia's distorted thinking, awful determination and willpower. Trying to persuade her to eat, knowing that if she doesn't that death could well be waiting, is the most agonizing and soul-destroying activity; despair is added to feelings of daily failure as Anorexia wins battles at meal times:

> The clinic say I have to make her eat, don't let her leave the table until she has eaten. I wish someone would come and show me how. I've tried explaining diet and nutrition – she can quote it word for word; I've tried cajoling and persuasion, threatening, even bribery – nothing works, we can sit there all evening and she just won't eat.
>
> (EDA helpline)

The following ideas come from a wide range of sources – my own, other carers, professionals. They, or adaptations of them, may help in your own situation:

- Make statements of fact like those below, but without any discussion and try to take the "personalness" out of the inter-action: *All breathing beings have to eat. There's no choice, we*

*have to eat too. This is what I've been told to do ... The dietician
says ... We need to make energy before we ... (walk the dog, go
shopping, whatever). Would you like A (perhaps a small sandwich) or B (a digestive biscuit with cheese) or C (a banana)?*
The choice is about *what* is to be eaten, not about *whether* to
eat.

- Leave small bowls of nuts or raisins, dried banana, crisps
  around – Anorexia may nibble.
- If ordinary meals are rejected, try offering milk shakes (low-fat
  milk, maybe whisk an egg in ...) or invalid drinks.
- If Anorexia is intent on cutting out food she believes will make
  her fat, but will accept a few other restricted items – it is better
  for her to eat anything rather than nothing at all, no matter
  how wrong Anorexia's thinking or how bizarre her eating is to
  your mind.
- If she insists on low-fat everything, no matter that you know
  ordinary bread or whatever will not instantly make her fat,
  allow her to have the low-fat item. If everything must be cut
  into minute bits, OK.
- Before mealtimes, try to think of topics to discuss at table,
  anything apart from food and eating.

**No matter what your own feelings or knowledge, the aim is
to keep Anorexia alive until her thinking can return to
rationality. Keep talking about how all living creatures, including Anorexia and Bulimia, need sustenance to live. All
activities need energy to fuel them. And don't give up if
something doesn't work the first time – keep trying. Your
daughter or son's life is at stake.**

Bingeing

When Anorexia's iron control finally breaks because her body is
screaming for food, Bulimia frequently takes over, causing huge
additional problems for families as well as for Anorexia.

Although the compulsion to binge is extremely strong, it is
possible for Anorexia and Bulimia, by applying that fearsome will-

power, to defeat the compulsion instead of struggling to cover up their activities or fighting with worried families and friends. It is possible for Anorexia and Bulimia to change things. Some families talk of physical battles to prevent bingeing, or at least to prevent the vomiting after a meal or a binge – guess who won? The compulsion can be so strong that if the bathroom is locked, Bulimia will simply find another way of disposing of the food, perhaps by visits to nearby, unsuspecting friends' houses. Physical "persuasion" as well as verbal battles simply don't work and cause more bad feeling.

It is therefore doubly important to help Anorexia and Bulimia to realize the damage such behaviour is inflicting on the body and to try to motivate, gently and persistently, toward change.

But, in the meantime, the family has to cope:

- *Forget about bulk-buying when Bulimia takes over.* Buying large amounts of food will simply encourage Bulimia to binge. For the duration of Anorexia's and Bulimia's stay – and that may be quite some time unfortunately – accept that more frequent shopping for smaller amounts will be necessary.
- *It may be necessary to hide some supplies for unexpected visitors –* tea or coffee, a few biscuits, some sugar, possibly some dried milk. This of course seems very underhand but is perhaps preferable to the awkwardness of offering a friend a cup of coffee only to find there is no coffee, let alone sugar or milk to go in it. Or biscuits. (I recently came across a small tin containing half a packet of biscuits, a few spoons of hardened coffee grains, stuck-together sugar, hidden behind some books. I laughed – and was thankful that I no longer need to do this to. I'd obviously forgotten the hiding place as my daughter began to recover.)
- *Suggest everyone serve themselves rather than allow Bulimia to pile plates high* (to disguise any difference between what she puts on her own plate and what others would normally serve themselves).
- *Make no comment if Bulimia piles her own plate* – it will only antagonize her, rather than make her eat a normal amount.
- *Try to keep table conversation away from food and eating.*

- *If you do come across Bulimia in the middle of a binge*, <u>withdraw</u>. At that moment, in the grip of such driving compulsion, Bulimia finds it almost impossible to stop, and your presence will make her guilt and disgust even more powerful. By staying, by commenting, nothing useful would be achieved. If there is an opportunity later, perhaps the fact that you know about the binge – and your own feelings – may be mentioned, giving Bulimia an opportunity to discuss how she felt and feels.

Kitchen organization

Can you organize cupboards so that it is immediately obvious when food has disappeared? In most kitchens, food is often kept in closed cupboards, in cardboard packets, tins and storage jars, so that it is only when some-one actually goes to cook that those packets, etc. are found to be empty. Which of course means that someone has to go and buy more food if the family is to eat ... :

- Try organizing your stores in transparent containers (big coffee or other jars?) on open shelves (see p. 114).
- Should Anorexia and Bulimia know of the problems their behaviour is causing for the family? **YES!!** By trying to ignore the effects on the family, by simply replacing the huge amounts of food, the behaviour certainly isn't being helped and could be seen as being condoned. If food vanishes try to find a way of stating that you have noticed, without having a row about it. No one said it was easy! Perhaps you could say something like *I love you very much and I know how difficult it is for you, but when you eat everything in the cupboard it makes it very difficult to organize meals for everyone else.* This lets Bulimia know that you've noticed food disappearing, you appreciate it's a problem for her and you think she's trying to control it. It also shows how it makes life difficult for you and others in the household. Above all, it shows that despite any

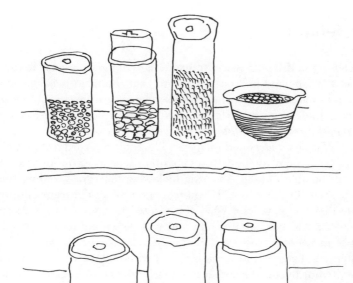

Figure 4 Transparent containers (big coffee jars?) for storing food will immediately show how much is there – or not. And knowing that might just give Bulimia pause for thought ...

and all difficulties you love her still. In the bleak world of Anorexia and Bulimia, this message is of enormous importance.

- No matter how much you try to keep calm, to speak reasonably, any responses from Anorexia and Bulimia as always will be unpredictable depending on mood. She may retreat into "hurt silence". She may burst into tears. She may rush up to her bedroom. Or Anorexia may well start shouting and screaming about no one loving her, no one understanding. And it is so easy to get drawn into a fruitless argument of trying to prove that on the contrary you as well as everyone else do love her ... Try hard to resist the temptation.

Listening

Listening is difficult when someone is irrational, but no matter what the tone and provocation try to hear the main message and reflect it back, perhaps in a single sentence. For instance, *You're upset because the curtains aren't pulled properly* or *You feel angry because I forgot which plate you like best* or *You're cross because you felt . . . I didn't understand you* (see "The broken record technique" on p. 126) You **may** (not always possible, depending on Anorexia's mood) be able to help Anorexia look at options for avoiding the same scene in the future. If Anorexia persists in the scene simply state that you have said what you wanted to say, and later when Anorexia and her pal are calm you will be willing to discuss the problem again. But now you are going to . . . take the dog for a walk, watch TV, listen to music, sit in your bedroom for a while, talk to a friend/your husband or other member of the family. Keep repeating that you love Anorexia and Bulimia and will happily talk over the matter later when everyone is calm. <u>Then go and do exactly what you said you were going to do.</u>

Kitchen and bathroom issues

Apart from table issues, bingeing can cause problems in the kitchen and bathroom. Sometimes Bulimia manages to cover her tracks quite successfully for a long time, finding times when the family are not around for her binges – perhaps at night or when others are not home from school or work – and leaving behind no mess. But if Bulimia cooks vast amounts of food, utensils and worktops will be messy and sometimes it is just not possible for her to clean up efficiently enough before someone returns. Again, the family has the dilemma of whether to say anything about the disgusting mess left behind in kitchen or bathroom . . . By ignoring the problem the family can set the scene for it to continue and get worse. And if the problem is not addressed it can indeed get worse, much worse. So, something must be said, no matter how risky it seems to voice your disgust, no matter how you dread a scene:

- Try to find a relaxed time, prepare and rehearse what you want to say and say it, as always stressing that it is the behaviour you dislike, not your daughter/son/partner. As always the reaction you get will depend on mood.

Mealtimes are fraught with difficulty for Anorexia and Bulimia

If you feel you really must discuss what you've noticed about Anorexia's or Bulimia's eating, try to find an opportunity away from the table. Try to avoid the subject of food if at all possible.

Now comes one of the hardest parts – What happens when all my/your efforts at the table have failed. I/you have allowed everyone including Anorexia and Bulimia to serve themselves, I/you kept eyes averted from her plate, I/you have talked of interesting topics and no one has said anything to disturb the atmosphere. And still Bulimia feels compelled to leave the table and visit the bathroom where you know exactly what she will do. To say nothing in this circumstance needs almost superhuman control (while for your daughter it will take almost superhuman control to defeat Bulimia's vicious control). This is the time to try to distract your thoughts, make that phone call, go walk the dog or whatever.

Specialist dietician

If your daughter has the good fortune to have contact with a specially-trained dietician with specialist knowledge of eating disorders, encourage her to talk about what the dietician said – listen very carefully and try to put into practice what is learned. (That's where I got the idea of thinking of topics for discussion at table, of avoiding talking about food or eating.)

Try to remember that this is your daughter's battle

In your daughter's battle for life against Anorexia and Bulimia, you can try to help:

- by trying to find moments for calm discussion when she feels able;
- by trying to keep calm in the face of great provocation;
- by trying to motivate toward change;
- by trying to find ways of convincing your daughter that she can indeed face life's challenges out in a big bad and scary world;
- by telling her that all the talents she has always had have not disappeared and are still there;
- by telling her that even though you can't accept some of Anorexia's behaviour you appreciate any effort she makes to beat Anorexia and you still love her no matter what.

But no matter how much you want to help, it is your daughter's battle and you can't fight it for her.

Budgeting

When my daughter became ill, she lost all the budgeting skills she had developed in her teenage years from making pocket money go round to running her own house for two years after leaving home to marry. Having given up my job, budgeting skills became an enormous issue when I began to realize just how much Bulimia's activities affected household life (see "Family areas affected by anorexia and bulimia nervosa" on p. 184).

Just as a young child, without any understanding of the concept of money, cannot comprehend *You can't have it because I can't afford it* when short-term wants rise to the surface, Bulimia cannot grasp that her eating and spending behaviour will affect her own budgeting ... and yours. As I realized that Jay had lost these skills, I felt it important to acknowledge the difficulties caused. Discussing budgets, both mine and Bulimia's, informally in response to various incidents became a regular feature in our house. *How much money was available? How could I pay this bill, would I/we have to do without something else? How much would each item cost in a catalogue? How much altogether? Can I/you afford it? The purpose of advertising is to* make *you want things so that companies can make money: Wow!, that really is a bargain at 25% off, that makes it only 75p, or £7.50 or maybe £75! But you wouldn't even have known about it if you hadn't seen – been sent? – the advert. So do I/you/we really need this? Is this the right amount, how much do I/we/you really need?* Gradually, with many setbacks, the lost skills were rebuilt and Jay's budgeting once again became realistic.

It would be great if a problem could be tackled by having a calm discussion that takes place only once, and then everything was better, the problem was solved. Unfortunately, in real life this is simply not realistic even with lesser problems, but with Anorexia it is probable that the same discussion over budgeting, kitchen or bathroom issues, whatever, will have to be repeated several – even many – times before progress is made. It feels as if you are stuck in a loop or on an endless conveyor belt that brings you back to the same place over and over again.

And it is exhausting, which is why families and in particular the main carer must work out other strategies for survival, because if the main carer collapses under the strain who is going to be there to hold things together?

Coping with the illogical, the irrational, the unreasonable

It took me some time to work out that there was really no point in trying to persuade by logical, reasonable and rational discussion if Anorexia could not think in a similar way – which was most of the time. When Jay was ill, there were days or weeks or even months when her thinking was so distorted that it was impossible to discuss anything at all in a reasoned manner. During those times, my daughter would explode at the least perceived provocation – a curtain not pulled "properly", a door shut or not shut when she wanted it otherwise, the "wrong" spoon laid out for her. At that time, lost in a very dark, miserable world, these incidents were taken as proof by Anorexia that her needs were not being considered.

Rocked by a rant?

There is little anyone can do when Anorexia or Bulimia goes off the deep end, into what can only be described as a rant. Trying to "prove" that you love her is impossible; no matter what you do or say will be wrong. Even trying to defend yourself, explaining that you didn't mean any insult, that there's been a misunderstanding, could make matters worse. Keeping calm under such an onslaught is incredibly difficult – but this is what carers must try to do. **Let it flow**. Try not to respond in anything other than a short calm comment, perhaps *Let's talk about this when you're calm again*. Keep repeating this until Anorexia has expressed all the anger and frustration she's feeling against the world in general – you're just the person who happens to be in the way at the time of the frustration. The less you say at the time the shorter the probable duration – if you try to talk it will most likely simply prolong the aggro. Gritting teeth, not responding to the provocation, will cause *you* stress, and you may need to go for a walk, listen to music, talk to a friend – anything to help you cope.

Waiting for a window of rational and reasonable thought is well worth the effort. When you can "grab the moment", be ready to talk calmly about what has been happening and how you feel – **don't ignore it**. Discussing what has happened gives Anorexia an opportunity to recognize how his or her behaviour has changed, how it affects others in the home – **and it could well be a beginning to recognition of problems and a motivation toward change**.

The "broken record technique" may help with this ...

The broken record technique

To say and keep saying what has to be said calmly and evenly needs practice. This is where talking to a good friend can help. If you are lucky you will have someone near; if not, a telephone helpline such as the EDA could help. Even practising in front of a mirror can be useful. Think out exactly what you want to say and how you want to say it. And then, when you feel ready, say it calmly, evenly – you must avoid ending up shouting. Angry shouting and arguments don't usually change anything with Anorexia or Bulimia, although sometimes it is necessary to show how angry and upset you are about behaviour that shows a complete lack of consideration and respect. In the face of hostility and rejection, constant manipulation and selfish attempts at control of all the lives around her, it would take a saint to refrain 24 hours a day from voicing feelings of rejection and hurt and legitimate anger at rude and inconsiderate behaviour.

But, when you are angry and upset is not the time to tackle problems with Anorexia or Bulimia. This is where the "broken record technique" comes in – this is a variation of a public speaking technique, taught to me many years ago at school in preparation for a debate, which I found very useful. **In public speaking, remember your audience and Stand up, Speak up, then Shut up.** In other words, say what you want to say clearly and calmly, then stop, don't witter on and spoil the original and important message you want to get over. Have an activity lined up for when you have said your piece and then leave the room, even the house, to carry out the activity. Leave your daughter to work out what she wants to do about the problem. Remember that your daughter's intentions may be different from those of Anorexia and her pal, who will always make every effort to control.

You will probably have to talk about the problem several times over a period of time – and any effort on your daughter's part to overcome Anorexia should be praised. It is so easy to forget to mention the small efforts, the small steps – if bingeing has been a real problem, then even a slice of bread left for your breakfast is a step forward; next time perhaps only half the loaf may vanish overnight. Accentuate the positive every time, eliminate the negative – you can only try!

Keep trying to feed in encouragement, build on and emphasize *any* progress; remember "Nothing succeeds like success".

How *do* you react to unreasonable behaviour?

Assertiveness

In the face of aggression, manipulation, hostility, rejection and unpleasantness, assertiveness is often difficult, especially if you have never encountered such extreme behaviour and most especially if you have never encountered it in your daughter (many people who develop Anorexia are reported as having been unusually compliant and quiet as children, but this is not always the case).

It is not easy to cope with Anorexia's behaviour, let alone accept that Anorexia, with or without Bulimia, has moved in with your daughter. Anorexia and Bulimia have very different standards of behaviour from those you thought you taught and tried to show by example. There may have been rows in the past about untidy rooms, or perhaps about coming in late, but your daughter's behaviour is now way beyond anything of the past. It is even more scary that it may occur at unpredictable times, over something major like bingeing or another food issue, but equally over something totally trivial such as Anorexia being handed the wrong mug, the curtains not being properly adjusted. Every tiny thing, a perceived wrong word or action or facial expression, is taken as proof of no one loving Anorexia or Bulimia. At its worst the aggression is frightening.

The unpredictability means that there is no way of knowing what Anorexia's reaction might be at any given moment, which is why many families simply allow Anorexia, often ably abetted by Bulimia, to take over. It is obvious that their daughter is very ill and her thinking distorted, especially about food and body image but about other things too, but they have no idea whether this is something they simply have to accept because of the illness, or whether they can do anything to change things.

There are many books (as well as teachers) on assertiveness and on communication. See the reference section – it is not exhaustive and you may find other books to help you or even a good teacher if you are lucky. Looking for practical books, talking to other carers, talking to people who have recovered, talking to someone on the EDA helpline – they can all help just as much as being lucky enough to find a good GP, a caring and compassionate consultant. It's well worth the effort of seeking them out.

Effective words ...

I beg your pardon?! (a teaching technique)

Four little words that may help (note the *may*, because Anorexia's mood is what will dictate her reaction): *I – beg – your – pardon?* Said with equal emphasis, the words are a simple request for repetition. If Anorexia has been rude, the request for repetition may just be enough to make her realize that she sounds rude, and she may not want to repeat her words. Now try saying these words with different emphases. How does it sound if you stress *beg*? I *beg* your *pardon*? What about I beg your *pardon*? Finally, *I BEG YOUR PARDON*???!!! Now add in your own bold type, maybe some underlining. Flashing eyes and strong body language too ...

Practice in front of a mirror – start with the mildest emphasis. When might you use this? Try all the suggested combinations. When might you try those? Can you see yourself using the most forceful emphasis? At full strength, with all the assertiveness you can muster, these words can be really powerful. And may even give pause to a "full-blown, over-the-top, out-of-control Hairy Jamaica!" (my daughter's description months later of an anorexic rage). Worth a try?

I love you very much, but ...

When you've had to cope with a "Hairy Jamaica", full-blown or minor, whatever it is about, **don't ignore that it happened**. Later, when things have calmed down, find a time to say *I love you very much but I really don't like it when you ... (name the behaviour) and shout at me as you did.* Anorexia or Bulimia may or may not be able to apologize but at least you have given her the opportunity to do so, and you have let your daughter know that you still love her no matter how Anorexia and her pal have behaved. If you find the behaviour distressing, even frightening, your daughter probably does too and needs your reassurance more than ever. By saying this, you are also giving Anorexia herself the opportunity to find a way of making a change to her behaviour.

I can see how difficult you find it but I'd like you to try hard to ...

Use this phrase as a prefix to such statements as *Leave enough food for your brother's breakfast.* This not only acknowledges that you appreciate that Bulimia has problems with the compulsion to binge but also states that her behaviour is causing problems for other people. It also gives the message that Bulimia can only try her best, and that you hope she will indeed do this.

Try to say what you mean and mean what you say

Try never ever to make promises or threats you can't keep or don't feel strong enough to follow through. *If you do that again, I'll throw you out!*, followed by ignoring the whole incident leading up to the words, gives very very mixed messages. If you do get to the stage of making such a threat, try to find a way of talking at a calmer time about what brought you to such a stage and such a final threat. Try again to say *I love you very much but I find your behaviour so difficult to cope with. I get very angry and upset by it. In future, please try not to ...* (talk about whatever it was that drove you to the threat in the first place). Doing your best and trying your hardest is all you can do, remember. Also, remember, you can't make Anorexia or Bulimia do anything – but neither can Anorexia or Bulimia make you do anything you really don't want to.

I'm sorry ...

It takes guts to be able to admit mistakes, much easier to try to ignore them and hope no one else has noticed them. Unfortunately, others usually do notice, and by not admitting to them you might give the message that's it's OK to deny what we have done or said or even thought. No matter how hard anyone tries, in life it is simply impossible to be endlessly controlled, polite, non-judgmental, cool, restrained ... and if you suddenly find yourself in the heat of the moment giving way to irritation, anger or any other uncomfortable emotion and say things you regret, it's better to "bite the bullet" and say how sorry you are. If you are willing to say you're sorry, perhaps Anorexia or Bulimia will eventually be able to admit that they too make mistakes and maybe they could try to change a little.

I really like it when you ... (and) Thank you for ...

As with praise, accentuate the positive whenever possible. For most people it's nice to be thanked for some small demonstration of care (e.g., putting out the dustbin even though it's a regular job they do), but for Anorexia and Bulimia in their bleak world of believing that they have nothing to offer anyone, that no one could possibly love them – it is extremely important to draw attention to any positive action you notice. A few examples:

- Thank you for bringing in the washing.
- Thank you for remembering to put your dishes in the dishwasher.
- Thank you for putting away your shoes.

And so on. What you are doing is telling someone that you notice efforts, even small ones often taken for granted.

These are a few ideas to try, I am sure there are others you can think of. The most important message, which Anorexia and Bulimia have huge difficulty hearing, is *I love you*. Keep saying it whenever you can, no matter what. And remember that finding a way of resisting all the aggression, all the manipulation and threats, in the face of such skilled operators as Anorexia and Bulimia, would tax the patience not to mention all the skill and talents of a saint. You, like me, are human, only human.

16

Coming up for air – stress, distress and survival for carers

As seen earlier with Anorexia and Bulimia, so too with carers – reactions to stress are individual. What is stressful to one person, say a row with a colleague, may possibly give that colleague a buzz! The first person is left trying to pick up emotional pieces possibly during sleepless nights, while the colleague instantly dismisses, even forgets, the whole incident and moves on without a thought.

In life we face all sorts of stress on a daily basis – financial, emotional, health problems, organizational. In today's world, despite all sorts of inventions that were meant to make life easier, pressures and personal expectations seem to be growing rather than diminishing. For instance, piped water saves fetching it for bathing and cooking; the vacuum cleaner makes house-cleaning easier; computers make communication easier; washing machines save us hours standing in front of a sink washing and wringing; tumble driers save us the trouble of getting clothes dry; the iron makes our clothes wrinkle-free with little effort ... All these were designed to save time that could then be used in more pleasurable pursuits.

This they did – but they also increased pressure and expecta-tions. Instead of having extra hours to follow our hobbies or to spend with our friends and families, we find ourselves trying to fit ever-increasing demands and expectations into the same number of hours. Because it's now possible to shower daily, it's expected that all members of our society *must* be clean and odour-free, it's antisocial to be otherwise; washing machines mean our clothes must be the same; our homes *must* be hoovered frequently, each room must be seen to be decorated, furnished and cleaned to a standard never before known, and advertising is designed to keep us up to date with "the latest" decorating and cleaning fads and gadgets; email as well as making it easier to keep in touch has meant that we can immediately receive such information as newsletters in an organization and has meant that many people expect instant answers, sometimes on a daily basis, where in the past snail mail meant several days between letter and reply; it's not acceptable to appear in crumpled clothes, etc.

There have always been stresses in life, in whatever society or community. There always will be. Cavemen had the stress of keeping warm, finding shelter and catching or picking enough food every day, just as the few primitive societies left on Earth today do. Some stress is beneficial – for instance, if the adrenaline rush caused by meeting a wild grizzly bear didn't energize someone into taking action, death might well be the next stop. In dealing with people we find difficult, the same applies (although thankfully death isn't likely to be a frequent outcome!). In this kind of stress, our hearts race for a while and then we calm down as life resumes a more tranquil beat. It is only when stress is ongoing and unresolved that we begin to feel its long-term effects in sleeplessness, possibly health problems, irritability, mistakes at work, at home and driving ...

Finding ways of coping with whatever stresses us personally is essential if we are to avoid or at least lessen its effects on our daily lives and allow us to go on functioning effectively. Even a short time each day of "doing our own thing" is valuable, but if you can find half an hour or a whole hour, daily or twice a week, it will give greater benefit. Let others cope for a while, and if there are any complaints because you were always available in the past say how important this is to you and that you'll be more able to listen properly to them and their demands if they let you have this space – and keep saying it. Remember we're talking about your survival as well as that of your family.

In 1999 I came very very close to cracking completely. Over

the previous three years I had watched my daughter gaining weight slowly and, despite her endless worry about her shape, slight curves were appearing. She looked better, much better, even though she'd refused any treatment after the initial few sessions, which led to a suggestion that at such a low weight and at risk of a heart attack because of low potassium she should be admitted to hospital. After that suggestion she stopped attending the therapy sessions. (She said she didn't need any therapy, what did the nurse-therapist know?!)

At the beginning of 1999 I really thought Jay was making progress and I had worked out all sorts of things, like it being counterproductive to comment in any way about her eating or food, how to cope with the rages. Then, overnight, everything changed drastically. Anorexia took over with a vengeance, and there was no respite for months. After eight solid months – May to December – of Anorexia's very worst behaviour – endless screaming and shouting over the least little thing, frequent threats of suicide *because no one loved her, least of all her mother, who couldn't even remember which mug she liked or if she liked the kitchen door open or closed, and the curtains properly drawn!* – I was exhausted and felt I'd run out of any ideas of how to cope, what to do. At the end of my tether, I felt I had tried everything I could think of, I'd even believed at the beginning of the year that things were improving, but then . . .

Each day I got up wondering what would happen that day, what I would have to face and try to cope with, if Anorexia would indeed carry out some of her awful threats – *and then you'll be sorry!!* The complete unpredictability of Anorexia's moods threatened to overwhelm me.

I decided to grit my teeth over trivial things – change the mug, shut or leave open the door as she wished at that minute – and realized trying to reason with Anorexia was impossible. So, I decided to concentrate on the big issues. With each incident I would ask myself *How much does this matter? How important is this?* Anorexia wants a different mug/door open or closed/curtain pulled or opened, whatever? – not important. No food for breakfast?!!! That was important, very important . . .

Sometimes I got so angry I could have exploded, but having concluded that retaliating angrily to provocation only sparked

Anorexia's already short fuse and having worked out that Anorexia couldn't hear or feel expressions of love, I tried hard to follow the line of *I love you very much, but I don't like it when you ...* Whether I had been angry or not, I tried always to say that it was because of my love and concern and fears, because I cared, that I had brought up the earlier behaviour. Often Anorexia began yelling no matter how I tried to express my feelings calmly and reasonably. Often, with fast-beating heart I would bring up earlier behaviour – that I didn't like it when Anorexia shouted at me, especially when all she had to do was ask for a different mug, etc., if it was important to her. Often I felt physically ill.

Where was Jay? I couldn't recognize Anorexia who had taken over; even her face looked different from my daughter's.

There were still moments of calm, but they were very rare. On one occasion, after weeks of struggling to cope, knowing that whatever I did was going to be seen as wrong no matter what the intention, the phone rang. A friend was phoning to tell me her good news. I talked to her – oh, the pleasure and delight of having a rational and pleasant conversation! – for a while. Suddenly Anorexia's angry voice came on the other line, *Typical! You knew I had a hair appointment at 2.30 p.m.! And now I've missed it because of you!!! You said you'd take me over at two!!! All you do is think of yourself.* When I told her that if she took the car she'd still make it in time, she still raged on and on about me forgetting. My friend asked if she should phone back. I said: *No, Anorexia could take the car herself and I'd do my shopping later ...*

A moment later, the door burst open and Anorexia began to yell and scream incoherently into my face, at which point I put the phone down and stood up. Apart from being absolutely exhausted from months of struggle and misery and not sleeping, I was really really angry. After the row Anorexia stormed out – and took the car to attend her hair appointment.

Later on, I brought up the incident which had left me shaking – and Anorexia started yelling and screaming again about how little I loved her. Then quite suddenly the screaming stopped, and my daughter looked at me. Her body sagged and Jay's face appeared, to replace Anorexia's which the moment before had been contorted with rage. *Can I have a hug Mum?* she said in a child's voice.

Braced against more aggression, I hesitated, then said *I'm sure that can be arranged*. As I put my arms around her, I said *Why?*

What do you mean?, my daughter asked, leaning into my shoulder, her arms wound tightly around me. I could feel how terribly thin she was, but thin rather than the emaciated bag of bones I had held a couple of years before.

It really upsets me, all the screaming and shouting. Why? I want to know why?

And she said in a frightened voice, *I don't know why Mum. I was out of control, over the top. I'm scared.*

For the rest of that evening we talked quite rationally, rare moments of calm and reason in a truly bleak year. The next day Anorexia came back.

Months later, after a difficult Christmas (with all that food around, Anorexia and Bulimia are bound to find Christmas difficult), the aggression and my exhaustion and limits of my endurance and patience all came to a head at the same time. A monumental row, with all the very worst features of everything that had gone before, led to me saying, *I've tried to understand, I've tried to make allowances, but if you really can't accept that everyone in this house has rights as well as you and won't even try to think about other people, then perhaps you should think about finding other accommodation*. And I meant it.

The response was instant. *You don't care, you don't understand, I'm going to kill myself!* Anorexia stormed upstairs, only to appear shortly afterward with a box of pills in her hand. *I've taken these and now I'm going to throw myself in the harbour. You'll never see me again. And you'll be sorry!!* The slam of the front door made the house shake.

I phoned the doctor, who was calm and reassuring. Had we had a row? Had this happened before? Did I know what she had taken? It's probably not a serious attempt ... Phone if she doesn't come back ...

As far as I knew there had been no pills in the house, but I didn't know what Anorexia might have bought. The next two hours were agony and I felt physically sick as I waited. The minutes felt like several lifetimes. I heard nothing except the sound of the wind getting up outside. Then the dog raised her head and her eyes followed sounds upstairs and I realized someone had come into the house.

I went upstairs with my heart thumping – and found Anorexia in bed. I shook her and asked what she had taken. Drowsily, she said she'd taken some migraine pills. When I phoned the doctor again, she reassured me that she would just sleep off the effects.

Three days later, my daughter told me that she had decided that she needed professional help to beat Anorexia and that she was sorry about everything that had happened. This was the first time since she told me of the diagnosis that she had been able to really acknowledge the depth of the problems and to say sorry for the effect Anorexia had had on me and my life. And we wept together.

No matter how deeply you love someone, no matter how rational and reasonable you try to be in pointing out other people's feelings and rights including your own, Anorexia is beyond reason, does not hear or feel your concern and love and despair. And it is extremely exhausting for anyone trying to cope, let alone keep calm. Anorexia would try the patience of a saint – and all the carers I know are human.

It is essential for carers to look after themselves, to think consciously of ways to survive. If the main carer goes under, what will happen to your daughter?

On every airline notices can be seen reminding parents travelling with young children to put on their own mask first in the event of an emergency. It took me quite a while to work this out in relation to life with Anorexia ...

A certain amount of stress can be positive – for cave-dwellers it was essential to survive! With adrenaline flowing, alertness improves as well as reaction times, decision making is faster, attention is in sharper focus. Today nobody faces sabre-toothed tigers, but just think of an interview or other situation when you felt it was really important to do your best! It is when stress – or rather distress – builds up and goes on for longer than a short time that it will eventually cause real problems. Living with long-term stress has effects that are recognizable and have been well documented, and the advice from psychologists and trainers is **Manage your stress or it will shorten your life!** With the average duration of anorexia nervosa being several years, this advice becomes crucial to preserve the physical, emotional and mental health of the carers.

And remember, **if the carers go under, what will happen to Anorexia?**

At its best, home is our haven from the Big Bad World out there, with all its problems. But family problems – including breakdowns in communication which may involve differing ideas, lifestyles, opinions, varying reactions to situations and behaviour – are a major cause of high stress levels. When Anorexia comes to visit a family, stress levels soar. Families trying to cope with Anorexia not only have to cope with the pain of watching as a beloved member begins to physically disappear before their appalled, distressed and uncomprehending eyes they also have to cope with dramatic changes in behaviour. **Recent research showed that stress levels in people caring for those with anorexia nervosa were significantly higher than people caring for those with psychosis** (Janet Treasure et al., 2000)

A few years ago, I attended an excellent workshop on Stress Management. The main speaker was a well-known Aberdeen psychologist Dr E. McCormack. As I listened, I began to recognize some of my own feelings.

I learned that stress signals include:

- *Physical effects* – changes in breathing rhythm, tense aching muscles, headaches, sweating, cold hands and feet, changes in appetite, stomach problems, palpitations, vulnerability to infections, flu, etc., blood pressure problems, nausea, dry mouth, sex difficulties, visual disturbance, cold sweats, clammy hands . . .
- *Mental effects* – lack of concentration, more frequent mistakes, forgetfulness/ absentmindedness, poorer judgment (all of which will affect work and driving as well as the rest of your life), loss of humour . . .
- *Emotional effects* – nervousness, depression, crying, anxiety, guilt, irritation, feelings of shame and failure, poor self-image, helplessness . . .
- *Behavioural effects* – insomnia, increased drinking/smoking.

Recognize any of them? I certainly did.

Once you become aware of the effect Anorexia is having on your own health, it is important to take positive steps to combat the effects of living with long-term stress.

Don't ignore them and hope they'll go away, they won't until Anorexia leaves your house and your daughter alone.

Make a list of what might help you and look for other things you may not have tried before. Then actively plan how to include these things in your life. In my case, the first things I thought of were music, walking, reading, later tai chi qigong, writing, planning at least one meal out of the house every week, an overnight stay once a month or so – sometimes I booked into a B&B because if I'd stayed with friends I'd have to relate to and talk to people. And I was just too tired to talk to anyone at all. Here are a few ideas to start you off:

- *Phone the Eating Disorders Association (EDA) helpline* – talk to others who are going through/have gone through similar experiences.
- If possible, *try to find a support group* where you can talk about all the frustrations and misery you feel, about your feelings of helplessness and despair and being overwhelmed by the illness in the darkest days. Talking to others who have gone through the same or similar, and come through to the other side, gives hope for the future as well as active support.
- *Tell your GP how you are feeling* – be prepared to change your doctor if you feel uncomfortable about discussing family problems and their effects, or if you feel he or she is unsympathetic.
- *Time away from home on a daily, weekly, monthly basis.* The daily break may only be a coffee with a neighbour or walking the dog, but that hour is important as a breather for you (as well as the dog!). The weekly break might be a meal with a friend, a concert or play, a drive to watch the sunset, a pub visit … And the monthly or three-monthly or six-monthly break could be a night or weekend away with your partner in a hotel or B&B or tent, visiting friends or relations, or a retreat. *The Good Retreat Guide* gives a huge variety of recommended retreat ideas and places, both spiritual and secular but all offering peace and quiet.

If Anorexia makes vociferous objections about being rejected – which she may do – listen to her and keep on saying that you need to have a break, to relax, you're sure she'll cope for a night or two. If you feel very uneasy about leaving her, perhaps a family member or friend might stay for the time you're away? It's very important that that person knows just how difficult things can be and when you'll be back. Even consider paying a qualified nurse if necessary. Not everyone is in the financial situation to afford this, but it is a possibility to be considered if there is no one else; and perhaps a social worker or GP might know of a respite fund to help? Don't let Anorexia control you and make you feel so bad that you give in again to her demands. If you give in, it'll happen again. And again. Make sure she knows when you'll return, say you'll contact her when you arrive ... And then go. Make sure you do exactly what you said you would, contact her on your arrival, return when you said you would. It will be easier next time.

Relaxation is difficult under stress and breathing is often affected by becoming very shallow. Neck and shoulders, chest muscles frequently feel tight and ache. Find a quiet time and place each day – even five minutes will make a difference, but half an hour is better. Sit still and breathe quietly, becoming conscious of the air moving in and out through your nose. Count up to three, then five, then six, seven, ten, each time you breathe in and each time you breathe out. Now try breathing in through your nose, sighing as you breathe out through your mouth. Count as before. Then as you continue breathing slowly and deeply and quietly, instead of counting repeat the words:

> *In – Out,*
> *Deep – Slow,*
> *Calm – Ease,*
> *Rest – Release ...*

This can be done anywhere, at home, at work, on the bus, in a traffic jam, on the train, walking to the shops. Close your eyes and try it.

Stretching to release tension can also help. Consciously tighten and then relax each part of your body, your neck and shoulder muscles, your face (make the most grotesque face you can think of and think of Anorexia who has taken over your life!), your arms, your hands and fingers, your back, your buttocks and thighs, your legs, your feet. Then s–t–r–e–t–c–h ... Do this as often as you like. Try "Relax plus" on p. 146.

A personal haven

Somewhere to retreat to for quiet and space is <u>really</u> important, perhaps on a regular basis as part of your day, certainly when things feel fraught and a cooling off period is needed. Try to find somewhere at home where you can be completely alone, perhaps your bedroom; arrange to have the bathroom for a long soak; if you have a spare room set it up for a hobby (e.g., sewing, reading, writing, painting), if not, go out to the shed; build a shed if necessary . . .

Music

Music has long been recognized as a great way of helping us relax, pulling us up when we're feeling down, soothing us as well as babies to sleep, helping us to address distressing events. Recently, the "Mozart effect" has been noted, where the brain can be stimulated into creative activity for a time. Not everyone is fond of music, a few people positively dislike music as they hear it only as irritating noise, but for many people finding particular pieces of music that suit their needs is very worthwhile. Many libraries lend CDs; so, it's not necessary to buy them until you find those pieces that work for you. These are my own favourites, which you might like to try:

- *Had a row?* Try Beethoven's *Emperor Concerto*, turned up loud, while you tackle a physical job. The crashing chords at the beginning may echo your own pent-up anger which you can express while washing the kitchen floor or hoovering or painting the spare room vigorously or any other physical activity – possibly accompanied by your tears. Then the later gentle flowing music may lead you, frustration spent, into a more peaceful frame of mind.
- Try dancing to Abba, put your whole energy into the dance, maybe while dusting and cleaning! Or skip the housework and just dance. Who cares if anyone laughs? – invite them to join in . . .

- *Tired and feeling low?* Try *Agnus Dei*, with the choir of New College Oxford; Vivaldi's *Gloria*; Albinoni's *Adagio*; Pachelbel's *Canon*.
- *Weepy and miserable?* Try Roy Orbison's "Golden Days" to help you let go of all that pent-up emotion.

There are many many other pieces of music – try to find what suits *you*, and make time for listening. Plan time for it if you find music works for you. Think about how you feel and what you need to work through. Use your feelings to guide you.

Exercise

Exercise is not only very important for our bodies physically but also for helping us relax emotionally. Find an exercise you enjoy, perhaps something you've enjoyed in the past, but consider trying something new. Any exercise is valuable – walking (a dog will listen to all your comments, will not speak back and will not betray a confidence!), swimming, tennis, dancing, aerobics ... Consider joining a class, which would give you the opportunity to exercise, meet people and have a break from home.

Hobbies

Hobbies are often dropped when people are under stress. Think about what you used to enjoy doing in the past and **make time** for it, whether it's knitting or woodwork, painting or tapestry, reading, whatever. Or look for something new – is there something you've always fancied trying? Find a class if possible ... surely the household can do without you for a couple of hours a week? If Anorexia objects, ask a friend or family member to sit in. Again, make time for it.

Writing

A powerful way of expressing and addressing feelings is writing, and it doesn't have to be shared with anyone if you don't want to.

Writing has long been recognized as a good form of therapy and it may just work for you. Here are a few ideas you might like to try:

- *Try writing a journal.* Recording events daily, or from time to time, and how you feel about them can be useful at a later date. You may be surprised to find how things have changed and moved on.
- The *unposted letter.* You could try writing a letter to someone telling them how you feel, pour it all out – and then tear it up or burn it.
- *Stories.* Why not try writing a short story? Give your characters voices, describe them and their relationships. What happens to them? These characters and events may be heavily disguised or instantly recognizable. All sorts of happy or awful things can happen to them. In writing a story, you can be omnipotent and make *anything at all* happen ... Again, you may or may not wish to share what you write.
- *Poems.* Perhaps you might like to try writing a poem? Don't worry about "rules", just write what you feel.

The wonderful thing about writing is that you can say *anything*, make *anything* happen, share it or not as you wish – and it can make you feel better.

Friends

Friends become really really important in hard times. If you are struggling to cope with long-term stress, you may feel that it's unfair to burden your friends. You may feel that by talking about your feelings of inadequacy you will be judged wanting in some way. Some people find it difficult to cope with the distress of others, or may only be able to show support for a very short time. Some may prove to have been fairweather friends, and simply drift away and not be around. But many people are glad to feel they can be of help, to feel that you can trust them with your deepest feelings. By allowing others to know of our distress, of our worst fears, of what seems too difficult to endure, we are also saying that we too will be willing to share their own miseries when they arise.

A problem shared really is a problem ... well, perhaps not halved, but definitely reduced to a more manageable size. Try to find at least one or two people with whom you can not only scale the ups of life, but also fathom the depths. When you feel you really can't talk to your friend about a particular problem – you've said it all before – phone the EDA or the Samaritans. Don't bottle it all up until you explode and the fallout makes an unhappy situation even worse, or until you are in danger of complete collapse.

If you are very isolated with no friends or family nearby, or if you truly feel that you don't want to burden the same people with the same worries and fears yet again, perhaps you could consider finding a trained counsellor who might be able to help.

Look for new as well as known ways to help you relax and cope

Have you tried massage? There are lots of different types of massage, you could try them all! Aromatherapy? Yoga? Tai chi (there are different forms, but tai chi qigong is a series of breathing and stretching exercises with the same calming effects as yoga)? Meditation? Dance?

Keep remembering the two steps forward, one back – three steps forward, two back – ten steps forward, ten back – two steps forward, one back – six forward, five back pattern of the illness. As your daughter gradually makes progress in her battle against Anorexia and/or Bulimia, think back a year, two years, five years. Concentrate on the efforts made, on any progress no matter how small. If possible, talk about it, share it, with your daughter, tell her about it and how pleased you are.

And, above all, keep remembering about putting on your own mask first in an emergency. If you go under, who will be there to care and support?

Relax plus

Relax ...

Make yourself comfortable in a quiet room – or outside – where you know you won't be disturbed for a while.

Sit down, close your eyes and begin to breathe gently and regularly. Be aware of the air passing through your nose. Don't try to control it in any way, simply be aware of it. Rest like this for some time, breathing gently and regularly.

When you feel ready, begin to count your breaths: *one – two – three – four – five – six*. Now return to one, and begin again: *one – two – three – four – five – six*. Repeat this several times. If you find your mind wandering, simply notice the thought then return to one and start counting your breaths again: *one – two – three – four – five – six* ... Continue like this for some time, breathing gently and regularly and counting your breaths.

When you are ready, replace the counting with:

> *In – Out,*
> *Deep – Slow,*
> *Calm – Ease,*
> *Rest – Release,*
> *In this moment,*
> *Precious moment.*

Continue like this for some time.

Plus

When you feel ready, imagine you are sitting in a peaceful place, perhaps a place you already know well. It might be on a beautiful beach. Imagine your surroundings: Can you hear the waves? The gulls? What else can you hear? Can you see any boats or birds? What else can you see? Can you smell the sea? What else are you aware of?

Or it might be on a hillside. Can you hear the wind? What else can you hear? What can you hear or see or smell?

Or perhaps you are in a lovely garden, surrounded by flowers.

Choose your own place and carefully examine your surroundings. Imagine as many details as possible. Continue breathing gently and regularly. Feel the peace all around you: *in – out, deep – slow, calm – ease, rest – release, in this moment, precious moment.*

And more ...

When you feel ready, look at the path that leads to your special place. Try to see it clearly ... Is it sloping or level, through trees? How far can you see along it?

When you can see the path clearly, imagine a very wise person is coming toward you following the path. Is the person male or female? Short or tall? Old or young? This person is carrying an empty bag. Is the bag swinging in a strong hand or is it flopping on the ground, or perhaps over a shoulder?

Slowly the very wise person is drawing ever closer, until that person is beside you. She or he sits down beside you. Together and in peace, you rest there side by side for some time in silent companionship. Without words, the wise person understands all your sadness and pain, the extent of your misery, the painful heavy burden that you carry. Gently the wise person puts a hand on your shoulder, then opens the bag, invites you to give up your burden.

Into the bag you put whatever has been troubling you. You give up your burden, put it into the bag.

The wise person picks up the bag with the burden. The bag is really really heavy and needs two hands to haul it onto his or her back. Very slowly, carrying the bag with your burden, the person follows the path leading away into the distance. Watch as your burden is carried away. Watch how heavy the bag is, how difficult it is to carry. Watch until the wise person with your burden disappears.

When your burden is no longer in sight, bring your attention back to your breathing. Sit quietly for as long as you like, breathing gently and regularly, before opening your eyes: *in – out, deep – slow, calm – ease, rest – release, in this moment, precious moment.*

Some burdens are so enormous and you have carried them for so long that they may not disappear in one visit, in one bag. Return to your special place as often as you want to, watch for your special friend who carries the bag, let your friend carry your burdens, your pain and grief away.

Pathways to professionals

A chapter for professionals and carers working together

First steps – GPs

The first step in finding professional help in any illness is usually a
visit to a general practitioner. Unfortunately:

> *GPs often miss eating disorders in their patients – because
> the patient may not ask directly for help.*
>
> (Dr Deborah Waller, GP, personal contact)

Eating Disorders Association (EDA) estimates that in an average
GP practice there will be 1–2 patients with anorexia nervosa, 18
with bulimia nervosa; between 5 and 10% of young women attending surgery will have eating disorders **and in 50% of cases the GP
will be unaware of it**:

> *The problem for GPs is not what to ask but when and how.
> Many may not "see" what is being presented or may too
> readily be complicit with the ambivalence that a sufferer
> may present. It is easy then not to take seriously enough
> what may be the early stages of an eating disorder and miss
> the opportunity to help. The first task is to take seriously
> what is being said.*
>
> (Dr Robert Mayer, GP, personal contact)

With thousands of possible conditions, illnesses and disorders – physical, emotional and mental – no single GP can possibly be expert in all of them. In many practices GPs offer expertise in a few areas which complement those offered by their immediate colleagues, make diagnoses, write prescriptions, make referrals on what they observe based on the answers to questions they ask of patients, on assessing what information they are given.

When trying to find professional help for anorexia or bulimia nervosa, several problems are immediately encountered. The main problem for both family and professionals is that whereas family and friends may be really worried by dramatic weight loss and change of character, being stuck in the "precontemplation" phase of the illness means that frequently neither Anorexia nor Bulimia admits to any problem (J. O. Prochaska and C. C. Di Clemente, 1992, p. 24). Not surprisingly, some GPs may be dismissive when Anorexia is brought to surgery against her will or simply to please her parents – then airily says there's no problem, it's all down to, for instance, her mother's fussing. Not surprisingly, some GPs then try to reassure the mother that all will be well, Anorexia will grow out of it. Or perhaps surgery is running late and the GP is simply irritated by "an overprotective mother" taking up his time with groundless worries. Amazingly, this phase of complete denial may continue even when Anorexia is skeletal and obviously weak from lack of sustenance:

Dr Harrassed: *I've taken your height and weight – you are a bit light. As a teenager you must eat a good diet, you're still growing ...*

Anorexia: *I really don't know why Mum brought me ... she's always fussing!*

Dr. Harrassed: *Look, I'll give you a Proper Diet sheet. Follow this and you'll be fine. Mrs Anxious Annie, you really must make sure your daughter eats a proper diet. Now, I've given Anorexia a diet sheet, all you have to do is make sure she follows it. Make another appointment in a few months' time and we'll see how you're getting on.*

The problem here is that in a few months' time Anorexia may well be so ill that recovery will be much more difficult, even almost impossible. There have been many instances where families have tried over months to alert a doctor – and been dismissed. In one case, a father at the end of his tether carried his daughter into surgery – she was too weak to walk – and asked the GP if he had to see his child die before anyone would take the problem seriously. The mother had already taken Anorexia to the GP on several occasions but had not been taken seriously.

In Bulimia's case (without Anorexia) she may often present at a normal, though possibly light, weight, having used binge and vomit and/or laxatives to control weight at what she considers acceptable; in this case there will quite possibly be no other signs of eating problems. And given all the other possibilities and pressures of time, not to mention Bulimia's reluctance to speak of problems and ambivalence regarding changing behaviour – probably agreeing with every word the doctor says while having no intention of following advice – not surprisingly, again, symptoms are not recognized, if disclosed at all. In the face of an apparently intelligent and compliant patient, a GP may dismiss family concerns.

In some cases, Bulimia reaches the "contemplation" phase of the illness and finally does admit to a problem, perhaps even makes an appointment herself, then chickens out of discussing the real problem – the effects of long-term laxative abuse perhaps, or she'll discuss the devastating effects on skin, teeth, hair of regular binge and vomit, but without mentioning the regular bathroom visits immediately after food. The family will often be only too aware of Bulimia's bathroom activities, but unable to find a way of making the doctor aware of the situation:

> *My daughter has been severely bulimic for six years, she abuses laxatives regularly as well as vomiting, to control her weight. Most of the time she looks great, sounds fine in company (not the case at home, her temper is often extreme over the least little thing!). Last week she came home in a state and told me she was bleeding heavily. I persuaded her yet again to go to the GP, and he did lots of tests but couldn't find anything wrong. She said she couldn't, just couldn't, tell him about her bulimia. She wanted me to go*

*with her, but he won't listen to me, just thinks I'm inter-
fering and ignores me. I don't know what to do, I think my
daughter's illness will have serious effects later on.*

(EDA helpline)

Not surprisingly, many GPs, busy with other patients who honestly and openly want to tackle their problems, don't pick up on
possible eating problems. Not surprisingly – but very unfortunately for Anorexia and Bulimia and their families. In Anorexia's
case weight loss, weakness and skeletal limbs may finally alert the
doctor despite what Anorexia says; with Bulimia, years of hidden
eating problems may result in long-term damage, even heart attack
as a result of low potassium.

The "precontemplation" phase and frequent denials cause
much frustration. So much depends on communication skills
between doctor and patient, being able to gently probe in a non-
judgmental way and offering Anorexia or Bulimia the possibility of
help:

*It also helps for the GP to be familiar with Anorexia and
Bulimia's strategies, which serve to discourage intervention,
and to make these explicit to the patient ... The single most
important thing is that the possibility that the patient may
have an eating problem crosses the doctor's mind – and that
she or he approaches the subject in a sensitive way with
some constructive suggestions for help should the patient
want it.*

(Dr Robert Mayer, GP)

Helpful questions for GPs to ask

- *Are you unhappy about the way you look?*
- *Would you like to be thinner than you are?*
- *Are you dieting?*
- *Do you feel you have lost control of your eating?*
- *Do you think you have an eating problem?*
- *Do you think you might be suffering from a problem like Anorexia
  or Bulimia?*

(Dr Deborah Waller, GP)

The more formal SCOFF questionnaire, which comprises five questions and was developed by the St George's Group, London, may also be useful in some situations for diagnosis:

- Do you make yourself **S**ick because you feel uncomfortably full?
- Do you worry that you have lost **C**ontrol over how much you eat?
- Have you recently lost more than **O**ne stone in a three-month period?
- Do you believe yourself to be **F**at when others say you are too thin?
- Would you say that **F**ood dominates your life?
- TWO OR MORE – LIKELY CASE.

If there is no eating problem, at least by asking a few gentle questions this possibility may be eliminated. If this is indeed the problem, the right approach may well allow Anorexia and/or Bulimia to talk about it and hopefully accept help for the first time:

The thing is to ask something rather than nothing.
(Dr Robert Mayer, GP)

For parents and other worried carers desperately seeking help, finding a GP who will listen and at least consider eating problems as a possibility is the first step in finding professional help for Anorexia and/or Bulimia. Having found a doctor with a listening approach, motivating Anorexia and Bulimia to accept help is often the next hurdle! Given the importance of a trusting relationship between patient and doctor, doctors are understandably reluctant to contemplate the possibility of breaking confidentiality by listening to a carer trying to give crucial information which may alert the doctor to undisclosed problems. However, by ignoring such information doctors then only have a part of the patient's health picture – and are handicapped in their diagnosis and future treatment. By the time Bulimia is willing to disclose problems, or Anorexia's dramatic loss of weight makes the presence of the illness obvious despite denials, the illness will be entrenched and much more difficult to tackle.

The earlier the recognition of eating problems the earlier help and support can be offered, and the sooner

those supporting Anorexia and Bulimia both at home and at the clinic can motivate the patient toward recognizing problems and accepting help, the less likely the illness will become chronic and the more likely the possibility of recovery.

If carers encounter GPs or other professionals who ignore their concerns and the information they wish to be considered, it may be a good idea **to write down their concerns and send them to the GP**. When a professional receives such information he or she may want to share it with the patient – who *may* vehemently deny its truth. On the other hand, the patient may be extremely relieved that someone has taken the step of giving the information she is so hesitant about presenting. Keeping a record of concerns and incidents may be very useful for doctors working with an ambivalent patient. It may also be helpful for families – and doctors – who can look back on it and see the progress made since it was written.

Next steps ... and referring on ...

Specialist help may involve a psychiatrist, psychologist, dietician, nurse–therapist – or any combination of these. In an ideal world on diagnosis of anorexia nervosa, in addition to individual meetings with the sufferer, there should be an invitation to a **meeting between parents/carers, professional(s) and an experienced carer**, preferably one whose family member recovered successfully. Sufferers may be invited if they wish to attend, but the meeting is mainly for families. Depending on staff availability, circumstances and numbers involved, such a meeting might be organized possibly two or three times a year for several families together, or only one or two families. There should also be a **family meeting with all members, including Anorexia and/or Bulimia, invited to discuss matters with the professionals**. Such a meeting can reveal a much wider, truer and more accurate picture of the real situation in the household, rather than a probably narrow and distorted view of one member, Anorexia.

By the time of diagnosis, families will have been living for weeks or months, even years, with high stress because of the sufferer's self-starvation, dramatic personality change, denial of problems, lying about food, possibly theft of money, etc. Under high stress, individuals react in different ways. Some may be tearful, others aggressive ... Many feel overwhelmed by the situation and desperate. Therefore, family relationships are likely to be fraught.

Aim of these meetings with families – to give information about the illness and to allow families to ask questions

Hopefully, these meetings will be the beginning of regular exchanges between professionals and families. Families can offer information about progress, professionals can offer encouragement, suggestions and, above all, hope. **Please tell it straight**:

- Anorexia nervosa (AN) is a serious illness with very serious physical and emotional aspects. It is often very difficult to treat as each case has individual differences, which means doctors have to find the right individual treatment.
- One of the most frustrating and difficult aspects of AN is frequently denial, often vehement, of any problems. With all thinking distorted, sufferers frequently cannot understand how ill they are.
- Prepare for a long road – the average duration of anorexia nervosa is 5–7 years, with many setbacks. Some sufferers recover more quickly than others, but unfortunately sometimes the illness becomes chronic, and because of self-starvation, mineral balances being upset, etc. it can be life-threatening.
- The sooner AN is recognized and treatment accepted the better the potential outcome.
- Two steps forward, one back; five forward, then five back; ten forward and several back ... is the common pattern. Each step may take months or even years.

Aim – to give useful telephone numbers

At the meetings, useful phone numbers such as that of the EDA and information about any local support groups/telephone support should be given.

Aim – to give a helpful reading list

At the meeting there should be a helpful reading list, such as:

- *Eating Disorder Association Carers' Guide*, published by the EDA in Norwich, UK.
- *Anorexia Nervosa: A Survival Guide for Families, Friends and Sufferers* by Janet Treasure, published by Psychology Press in Hove, UK.
- *Recovering Together* by Arthur Wassmer, published by Henry Holt in New York.

The last is for families of sufferers from alcoholism/addictions/compulsive behaviour, but is also very relevant to anorexia nervosa. Other self-help books connected with codependency, Alcoholics Anonymous and Al-Anon could also help.

Aim – to offer families ideas for coping

It may be helpful at the meeting for professionals to separate the behaviour of Anorexia from that of their beloved family member. Such ideas might include, if bingeing is a problem, forgetting about bulk-buying and buying only small quantities as well as storing food in glass jars on open shelves instead of hidden in cupboards. Families should be encouraged to share their own ways of coping (see Chapter 15).

Aim – to give families a role to play

In other serious illnesses (e.g., cancer) a care plan is drawn up and families and carers are seen as important caregivers, which reassures carers that they are doing everything possible. This, of course, should be the case for anorexia and bulimia nervosa, as well. The care plan should cover:

- *Motivation* is one of the most important areas where families and friends can try to influence sufferers to accept change is needed, that sufferers will be supported if they risk change.
- *Reassurance* ... When anorexia nervosa takes over, the sufferer cannot hear expressions of love; instead, they see an expression of concern as interference or minor irritations (e.g., being given the "wrong" mug) as proof that no one cares about them. A phrase such as *I love you very much but I don't like it when you ... scream and shout at me, or eat all the food meant for the whole family* may be very helpful – it reassures the sufferer that it is anorexic behaviour that is unacceptable and unloveable, not the sufferer.
- *Boundaries* ... Don't ignore unacceptable behaviour. Try to develop helpful phrases, such as the above, and practise if necessary.
- *Teamwork* is very important – talk to each other, share information, discuss problems and possible approaches. Set up weekly meetings around a table if necessary, with all family members there if possible to discuss achievements, problems, setbacks.
- *Accentuate the positive* **(anything at all, no matter how small)**, and eliminate the negative (see Chapter 15).

Aim – to ease the suffering of carers who blame themselves for the illness

Professionals at the meeting should reassure carers who find reasons to blame themselves: Is it because she's the youngest and maybe we indulged her too much? Is it because we sent her to boarding school? Is it because I was too strict, expected too much? Carers should be told about current research which points to genetic vulnerability, reactions to stress, etc.

Aim – to encourage carers to find support for themselves

If carers collapse with exhaustion, who will look after their ill family member? Remember – "When flying, anyone accompanying a child or invalid, should put on their own mask first." Professionals should advise carers to make looking after themselves a priority – to consider massage, meditation, a retreat and to continue at least one hobby outside the house (e.g., painting, music). Anything that gives a little peace and respite when living with a volcano (see Chapter 15). Professionals should encourage carers to look for what they feel they need (e.g., assertiveness training to help stand up to Anorexia's explosive rages) or to find someone to talk to – consider finding a professional counsellor if no close friend is available, or phone the EDA helpline, or find a self-help group, or start your own self-help group.

Aim – to give families hope

Professionals should stress that people can and do overcome anorexia nervosa and recover, and that with a lot of co-operation and teamwork the carer's own family member and the carer's own family can and hopefully will not only come through the experience of anorexia nervosa but emerge even stronger than before.

Aim – to minimize the distress of families, to encourage their efforts to motivate and support their family members and to maximize co-operation with professionals

In addition to individual treatment for sufferers, professionals should offer regular – every few weeks/ months depending on circumstances? – family meetings, with carers and sufferers invited as before, to review progress, discuss problems and outline next steps. They should encourage the keeping of journals – writing is a good way of expressing intense feelings, can remind you of progress or of questions that people want to ask at meetings.

Professionals should if at all possible ask Anorexia and/or Bulimia to involve at least the main carer in her treatment. **Who** *would you like to bring along to our first meeting to support you?* rather than *Is there anyone you would like to bring?*, giving the message that you are sure she would like to have a special person there as a support. That special support person may be a parent, another relative, a friend and could prove invaluable to a professional in forming a clear picture of progress or lack of it, as well as supporting the sufferer in her efforts to regain control.

Specialist dieticians

Specialist dieticians in eating disorders are few and far between and are worth their weight in gold. Many dieticians have no specialist training in treating eating disorders and apart from giving general information on diet and nutrition are at a loss when faced with Anorexia or Bulimia, who appears to listen and agree politely with all that is offered – then go home and carry on exactly as before.

If a sufferer is referred to a dietician with special experience in eating disorders, as my daughter was, Anorexia may well heed that advice and ignore any advice from anyone else. By listening carefully to what Jay said after one of these valuable appointments, I gleaned what had been suggested: that Jay try to build on the positive parts of her eating patterns; not to try to change everything, break all the bad habits, all at once overnight; and not to give up if she had a setback.

This translated into working out the meal – for Jay, breakfast – which was most likely to be retained and add perhaps a yogurt to that, then a little more. When that meal was established, work then moved onto lunchtime and together Jay and the dietician worked out what might be a realistic amount to eat without risking the absolute panic that would ensue if Jay felt she had eaten too much. A night a week was identified when Jay would remain with me at the table after a meal and not immediately visit the bathroom. Then two nights. Jay told me about the suggestion that whoever she ate with might try distraction through choosing interesting topics of conversation and I tried hard to come up with something each night ... Three nights a week binge-free, then four ...

Gradually, very gradually, Jay began to regain control of her eating. At first, each step seemed almost insurmountable – there were many times when all the efforts failed and Jay vanished to the bathroom. And I felt a failure in not being able to help her conquer the compulsion, which was so strong.

There were many many setbacks – remember the two steps forward, one back, three forward, three back? – but perseverance linked with determination and lots of praise for any ground gained eventully paid off. Jay may have lost some of the battles short term – but she won the war. The pace of progress grew as time went on until at last Jay's diet and eating were more or less normal. Very occasional binges still take place under stress, but Jay is obviously healthy and can even go out for a meal and eat more than usual of her favourite food, without panicking.

Encouragement (especially in the face of setbacks), reminders of what has been achieved in the battle to regain control of eating or behaviour and, in the event of a a setback, spoken appreciation of the obvious effort involved in regaining lost ground were all crucial in the fight and are the most important gifts family or friends can give.

For carers working with professionals

If anorexia or bulimia nervosa is diagnosed in the early teens – or even before puberty, which happens – families will be involved as part of the treatment, but this is not always the case when a patient reaches 18, the age of majority.

Sometimes, if Anorexia is over 18 when the illness develops, a carer may be invited to a meeting with a professional **if Anorexia is agreeable. Many professionals currently interpret the possible involvement of anyone other than their patient as**

a breach of confidentiality, despite evidence that points to enhanced outcomes of treatment by involving supportive carers. Anorexia may well refuse to allow carers to attend any meetings – possibly because she feels carers are fussing unduly; possibly because she wants to tell the professional her story without anyone else there; possibly because her deep unhappiness has its roots within the family and she doesn't want to talk about the situation in front of those involved; and possibly because she has told such a tangled web of stories to various family members that she fears reactions when these are found out.

Parents and other carers may be frustrated by the feelings of being excluded, especially if they want to help, and with Anorexia's distorted view of the world Anorexia's version of events may well not be accurate – **but the most important factor is that Anorexia is accepting help**.

Carers often have to rely on listening to what Anorexia wants to share – **if** she wants to share anything when she has seen a professional. No matter how a carer may feel, it is important to respect Anorexia's right to privacy. Simply be there, be ready to listen, show and tell Anorexia that your love is unconditional, you are there and ready if and when she would like to talk. The more you can demonstrate that you trust Anorexia and the less pressure to get her to divulge what happened at a session with a professional, the more likely Anorexia is to share feelings, hopes and fears – but for anxious carers, waiting and hoping can be agonizing. That's where it's important to make sure you have your own life, with activities outside the home, to take up at least some of your time and energy; unfortunately, it is all too easy to allow legitimate and long-term worry to chew you up and adversely affect your relationship with Anorexia.

Relapse . . . and avoiding it

When Anorexia takes firm hold and becomes life-threatening, sometimes hospitalization is the only answer. Depending on local health authority resources, treatment programmes vary widely, with the best offering not only individually tailored therapy but also structured activities throughout the day. Art, drama, writing, music ... all may be on offer to help address all the issues a sufferer may have to work through, as well as education on healthy eating and menu planning in preparation for returning home. Some clinics trust and encourage patients to go out to eat in a restaurant just before discharge, so that patients can support each other in choosing from the menu and eating a full meal in public.

Terry's story

Terry, 23, was looking forward to going home. Every weekend for the eight months she had spent in hospital her mum and dad had travelled the 250 miles to visit her and she knew they were looking forward to taking her home too. She felt so much stronger and positive about keeping up the eating programme the hospital had worked out with her. A couple of short visits home had been discussed with staff on her return, and everyone was very hopeful that this time she'd stay well, stay out of hospital. She would miss some of the girls, especially Katrina, but they were going to keep in touch. Kat would soon be going home too; maybe they'd arrange to meet up sometime.

Dad had redecorated her room specially for her; they'd chosen the paper while she was at home last visit and that was something else to look forward to ... Her own room in her own home ... Being able to get up when she pleased, go out every day with Conker, her horse, maybe start helping at the stables again ...

It would be hard, but she was sure she could do it this time. This time ... she felt a bit nervous about keeping up the programme, but knew that Mum would try to help her as much as possible. Yes, she was sure she could do it.

(Based on carer support meeting stories, names changed)

Sadly, despite all her efforts and those of her family (and friends and neighbours) to help and support her, Terry relapsed within a few months. So did Katrina, although she didn't relapse until 18 months later.

Katrina's story

In Katrina's case she decided to take a further year out of studying, got a job as a waitress and threw herself into making up lost time socially. The job was fun – she enjoyed meeting all the people in the hotel where she worked – and it gave structure to her days so that regular mealtimes were fairly easy to organize. Then she met Ian and life began to really take off. After a few months they decided to become engaged and share a cottage. Unfortunately, Ian was not as committed as Kat, and when he announced he wanted to move on to pastures new all Kat's efforts to stick to her eating programme fell apart along with her dreams. The job had been seasonal, as was accommodation in the hotel. Losing weight again, Kat decided to move back home. Contacting the specialist ED Unit where she had been treated in the past, she found that there was a year's waiting list to be seen ... and she was at the end of it.

Luckily Kat had a very good GP who was willing to listen and support, her family were very supportive and there was a self-help group locally; all helped her through the long wait for specialist help.

Terry's story (cont.)

Terry, with the help of her family, stuck to her eating programme for several weeks. Everyone was pleased to see her at home, friends phoned and arranged to come round or go out. It was wonderful to be able to spend time with Conker. Then mum went back to work, she couldn't take any more time off. Despite many letters and phone calls, Terry had been unable to find work and was on her own during the days when everyone in the family was out at work or school. Neighbours and friends popped in when they could, but they too had work and school and busy lives.

The days seemed to get longer and longer, and Terry found it harder and harder to stick to her eating programme without mum there to support and remind her. First she stopped having her mid-morning drink and snack. Mum tried to get home at lunchtime whenever she could, and lunchtimes continued as planned. The afternoon snack was abandoned next. Then Terry felt unable to eat with her family at teatime and, out of sight of her family, cut down on what she was eating. Feeling depressed at her perceived failure, and increasingly tired as her body began to miss nourishment and was unable to replenish energy, Terry often prepared to go to bed early. Mum would then remind her about her bedtime milky drink. Terry began to make sure she was in bed even earlier, deliberately avoiding that milky drink.

In the end however, the effort was too great for Terry. Anorexia took over again, as for Kat. Both unfortunately spent further time in hospital.

Although most hospital ED programmes include some sort of support in planning for eating with the family at home, eating at social gatherings, eating in public places and talk patients through different situations that might cause stress or anxiety, few offer support in any other way. Patients are frequently discharged to exactly the same home situation as they left a few months earlier, to family who may desperately want to help and support – but who are given no more guidance than they had in the initial stages of the illness and have little or no idea of what to expect. Families often think that because Anorexia has retreated and their daughter or son looks so much better, and sounds more like themselves again, that all problems are over. They think the patient is "better". They are right – the patient is indeed better – but not cured. A new battle is just beginning.

Patients sometimes go home for short spells, as Terry and Kat did before discharge, with the visits and any problems discussed on return. Then Discharge Day arrived and they left hospital – a highly-structured, safe and secure environment, organized to surround patients with care and the maximum in support. For instance, meals were eaten together, toilets were out of bounds afterward in case Bulimia was tempted and days were programmed and planned to be filled with activity and interest, all designed to help, support – and distract from thoughts of food or other problems.

On discharge, Kat was working and this gave her days a certain structure, but Terry was less fortunate. Although her family were loving and very supportive, they still had to earn a living, to pay bills. But unable to find work, Terry relied on her family for company. From having activities organized for her days in hospital, Terry found that after the initial weeks when her mother was able to take time off work, she faced long days of boredom and emptiness. Aware of her daughter's loneliness and depression at the prospect of Anorexia beckoning again, Terry's mother gave up her own interests if they involved being out in the evening and rarely met her friends unless they could come to the house, in an effort to offer the company missing during the day.

It was when Kat's carefully-built support structures – a job, regular hours, activities – disappeared that Kat relapsed. And for Terry, unable to find a job and without the rhythm of regular activities, relapse came quickly. This is an extremely common pattern ... unfortunately, with anorexia nervosa, once it becomes chronic, relapse can be a regular feature. For many with eating disorders, the return to real life – where other people have busy lives and hours filled with work, friends, hobbies, activity – becomes yet another battle. Not just the battle to beat anorexia or bulimia at mealtimes, but a struggle against boredom, lack of energy, lack of motivation or opportunity to find interesting activities or even to make contact with new or former friends.

In the ideal world mentioned earlier in this chapter patients would spend much longer in preparation for discharge. Not only would planning for the continuation of healthy eating habits be discussed in depth and a written plan be worked on, considerable time would be spent on working out what else real life will involve, all the possible – probable – problems that might be encountered

and how they might be tackled. A weekly plan discussed and
written down might make a huge difference to anyone in Terry's
situation when everyone else in the household was out during the
day at work or school and had a social life, all of which she lacked.
Such a care plan could well be the difference between coping with,
perhaps with a bit of a struggle at initial readjustment, and sliding,
as both Terry and Kat did, back into the clutches of Anorexia.
Quite apart from eating disorders, anyone who has spent some
time in hospital for whatever reason will recognize the importance
of the routine set by mealtimes, visitors, tests, treatments, X-rays,
physiotherapy perhaps, the safe, secure environment, no responsibility, with even the temperature controlled ... and the shock of
adjusting on discharge to being expected to make meals, possibly
being responsible again for organizing a household, climbing stairs
and sharing family life. For someone living alone, as many have to,
the luxury of a loving family – or even an exasperated but essen-
tially supportive one – is not an option and the trial of transition is
even greater.

So – what can be done?

Short visits home, extended gradually, might be possible for some,
but this is not always an easy option if families live hundreds of
miles from the treatment centre. For others, because of personal
circumstances, this is not an option at all. A "halfway house" with
support if and when needed, opportunity for activities and
company if and when needed, could make all the difference for
successful re-entry to real life. Discharge could then be planned
around this safe haven, with a support worker under the same roof,
where Terry could have spent a night, a weekend, a week, then
gradually longer, until she felt ready to cope with more independent living either at the family home or elsewhere. The halfway
house could comprise individual flatlets, with a communal kitchen
and sitting room perhaps and have access to some hospital activities on certain mornings/afternoons/days. As a planned progres-
sion from life on the ward, the halfway house should be considered
and discussed from the earliest days after admission as an integral

step on the way to regaining independence when strong and well enough to do so. Investment in such accommodation could act as a two-way stepping stone: on the one hand preparing patients for real life, and providing shelter when Anorexia is struggling in the real world to gain complete control and support is needed to avoid readmission to hospital on the other hand.

Discussion of detailed plans, perhaps even working out a week's timetable, about how to occupy time could be literally invaluable.

Relapse Management Cards

It is hoped that Relapse Management Cards will aid care and management in the event of a relapse or even play a part in diverting a relapse at an early stage.
(Lisa Page et al., 2002)

At the Maudsley Hospital, London, Relapse Management Cards have been filled in voluntarily by inpatients as part of investigations into how it might be possible to avert relapse by recognition of early signs. In a previous study in another part of Mental Health Services, "crisis cards" were thought to be useful in four major areas – providing information, enabling early recognition of relapse symptoms, as an advocacy tool and to allow for advance planning for care in a crisis – and the study (Sutherby et al., 1999) concluded that crisis cards might have both a practical and psychological function. In that study:

... the data studied suggested that admission rates fell in the 2 years subsequent to card completion. There may also have been positive effects on patients' attitudes to their illness and treatment and an improvement in their relationship with staff.

With ED patients at the Maudsley:

... over 77% of patients stated that changes in food habits would be an indicator of relapse and cited social withdrawal as a sign which might act as a good marker for both families and professionals. As many as 56% of patients

*felt they became depressed when relapsing, with one noting
"I become depressed, moody, eat alone and isolate myself
from others."*

With hundreds of miles between them, this description could have
applied to Terry when she began to suffer relapse.

The Relapse Management Cards outlined in the paper about
the work at the Maudsley were broken down into the following
sections:

- Treatment on discharge.
- Plans to decrease likelihood of relapse.
- Signs of relapse.
- Interventions which have been helpful in the past when
  relapsing.
- Interventions which have been unhelpful in the past when
  relapsing.
- Plans in the event of the relapse.
- Specific refusals in the event of a relapse.
- Reasons to be readmitted to hospital.

Patients who filled in the card, when asked to outline their plans to
reduce likelihood of relapse, included: identifying eating strategies
that might help (35%); involving family or friends in care (40/30%);
involving professionals in care (62%) and becoming involved in
work/study (42.5%). As for their plans in the event of relapse,
42.5% mentioned involving family and 70% involving professionals. Patients also identified the Body Mass Index (BMI) at
which they thought they should be readmitted.

Cards are completed by patients at a "facilitated family
meeting", after thorough discussion and no little encouragement.
With patients signing the cards while they are *well*, under the
auspices of a professional, this could be a very positive tool to
benefit patients if and when they relapse and could also help
families and professionals. This could prove a huge boon to
social work teams, who may or may not have been involved in
earlier treatment and are faced with Anorexia in physical danger,
emotional pain and quite possibly – probably, if Anorexia has done
her vicious work – in the "precontemplation" phase of the illness,
sometimes with no other information to go on.

With illnesses like anorexia nervosa that have such high relapse rates, *anything* that could benefit sufferers, families and professionals is worth investigation, consideration and development. Perhaps:

- if cards had been used in Terry's case;
- if before discharge a weekly timetable had been worked out, with the chance of voluntary work should no job be found;
- if her family had had more information or guidance and had recognized the beginning of relapse – onset of depression, withdrawal from family and friends and changes in eating habits;

- if early intervention and proper support had been available ...

... perhaps relapse could have been averted.

End of the story ...
or rather, a new
beginning ...

It was a nightmarish experience to watch my beloved Jay disappear under Anorexia's vicious grip. To watch helplessly as she became so thin that her skeleton was clearly visible, the skin on her pale face stretched taut over the bone structure, to see her so physically weak that she was unable to sit for long. Each evening she lay on the sofa because it was too painful to sit even on the padded upholstery, hip bones clearly visible even through her clothes. Her lovely figure vanished; most noticeable was the absence of a rounded bottom – clothes hung loosely over bone because all flesh was gone. Spots, never one of her teenage problems, erupted on her previously smooth skin, her hair was thinner, her hands were claw-like, rings sliding on the bony fingers. Jay's beautiful dark eyes were sunk into the sockets and took on a black staring quality I'd never seen before. And she was permanently cold, unable to get warm.

All these I now know are recognizable symptoms of anorexia, the body's response to lack of food being to close down non-essential functions in an attempt to keep the main organs going. Keeping the heart beating 24 hours a day takes a lot of energy even when sleeping soundly, let alone when walking, running, working, playing, and vital energy is conserved in any way possible (e.g., periods stop, teeth and nails became damaged).

To watch the devastating physical effects of starvation was bad enough, but far worse was the disintegration of Jay's bright personality. All confidence disappeared along with her sense of humour; laughter vanished from our house for a very long time, and for what seemed an eternity I couldn't imagine it ever coming back. No matter what reassurances were attempted she felt that no one loved her, no one could possibly love her. Rational conversation was impossible and ended, no matter what the subject, with, *You don't love me, you hate me!* Fierce, unpredictable irritation and quicksilver changes of mind over the most minor frustration became the norm, her tone varying from surly to insolent to angry, and frequently screaming and yelling (over things like the "wrong" spoon being laid at her place, the curtains not being drawn to her satisfaction, a pair of her white knickers accidentally going into a coloured wash load). Even an inadvertent look "in the wrong tone of voice" was enough to provoke a tirade about the imagined criticism or insult, let alone a real complaint about the state of the bathroom after Bulimia had spent time in there.

I now know that mine was not an unusual experience when Anorexia and Bulimia come to stay; in fact, from the helpline and meetings I know there are some aspects I haven't experienced. At the time I felt totally isolated, as if I was the only person in the whole world living in such a nightmare.

For a long time – until I found Eating Disorders Association (EDA) about two years after Jay finally telling me of the diagnosis – I blundered around blindly, desperately trying to find a way to reach my daughter in the increasingly dark and bitter world she seemed to be in, terrified that I might make things worse by saying or doing the wrong thing, unable to find any help or support or guidance. Any information I did find through books made me feel worse rather than better because, while damning parents as the cause of the illness, not one gave any indication of what parents had actually done or should be doing. I am infinitely thankful I didn't come across the worst of these writings at that time!

The last few years have witnessed many many setbacks, many lows, some depths I thought I'd never survive, let alone climb out of. Not only did I become afraid to trust any progress in case other steps were then taken backward I was also afraid to relax, which meant being even more vulnerable to Anorexia's attacks. The name of my house *Am Fasgadh* means "safe haven or harbour" ... it seems ironic that the only place I definitely didn't ever relax was at home. For about four years I had to go away from home for an hour or three, a day or three, to gain some peace. I look back, especially to 1999, and find it frightening to recognize how very close I came to collapse and wonder how I did indeed survive.

Once, before I finally gave up my job, I booked in for a long weekend retreat – a recognition of my state of total exhaustion. I looked forward so much to the time with other people who did not know me, to gentle activities spent with reasonable company. On the Friday evening I enjoyed a lovely meal and conversation around the table, then went to bed and slept like the proverbial log – the first time for months. The first activity of Saturday would start at 10 a.m. As there was no chair in my room, I lay down on my bed after breakfast to read ... and woke up at 4 p.m. having slept through the whole day. Determined to do better the next day, I went to bed very early, drowsy from the fire and listening to talk around me. Sunday, I ate breakfast, joined in the multicultural spiritual celebration and having an hour or so to spare before lunch picked up my book again. You're ahead of me ... yes, I slept the day away again, probably the most expensive sleep I've ever had! But next day, I did feel refreshed enough to face going home.

"May you live in interesting times!" – I've never been sure whether the old Chinese saying is a blessing or a curse, but I certainly feel I've lived in very interesting times as I followed the steep learning curve that has led me here – to writing this book. Having talked to many other parents in similar situations, I count myself fortunate to be able to watch Jay come back, to see her regain her confidence enough to decide to give up the repetitive job she'd done for the 10 years since leaving school, to go to college, to choose what she wanted to study.

There seem to be varying degrees of the illness, just as there are in other conditions including cancer, diabetes, epilepsy, asthma and other illnesses that can be life-threatening, and sometimes despite all sorts of attempts at support from families, from friends and from professionals, Anorexia wins. A few people seem to be able to defeat Anorexia within a fairly short time, a year or two perhaps. Others with little professional input are able to slowly regain control of their lives. Beating the illness may depend on early recognition of the problems and prompt treatment by a specialist with experience and compassion, or perhaps on the strength of will of the sufferer and the determined support of whoever she lives with. But I know that in some cases the struggle goes on for many years, with distraught families and frustrated professionals equally helpless in the battle with Anorexia. In these cases the sufferer may take many steps forward and back, as if in some ghastly dance, before dying of heart failure or perhaps mineral deficiencies caused by lack of proper nutrition or perhaps by committing suicide rather than face any more pain.

I know because I have spoken with parents who have lost their children, who have had to come to terms with the memories of behaviour that was Anorexia's and not recognizable in any way as the loving and loveable child they had brought up. In one case the parents were completely rejected by Anorexia, despite her acknowledgment that they had always done their best for her. And these are just two of the cases I know personally, but these tragic family stories are repeated in homes all over the world.

So, I count myself very fortunate. My daughter may struggle, at times of stress throughout her life, with the destructive effects of Anorexia's whispered messages and stranglehold, but having come through the last few years Jay has shown her determination to fight off the illness.

Looking back I feel several factors were blessings in very heavy disguise. Not long after I left work, I had to go into hospital for an operation. There were a few complications and I was in hospital for two weeks during which Jay visited frequently. She looked like a walking skeleton and one or two nurses commented that perhaps they should prepare a bed for her too! Being away for that fortnight showed me that whatever she said, **Jay could cope without me**. It may have been a struggle – she certainly didn't like me having time out of the house when she wanted me there and did her utmost in every way many times to "persuade" me to change my plans – but she could cope.

And the fact that my hearing problems meant that I could literally "switch off" during the worst "Hairy Jamaicas" rather than being drawn yet again into trying to show that I did love her, no matter what Anorexia kept saying in my daughter's head – that ability to "switch off" was a definite advantage many times!

How did I know Jay was recovering? What signs did I recognize as Jay returned home? Looking back I can see that gradually Anorexia went on longer and longer holidays until at last she rarely visited; when she did show her face after an absence of perhaps weeks, she was recognized, dealt with sharply and retreated.

Laughter was one of the main signs of Jay's return. I didn't realize how much I had missed Jay's sense of humour until one night I repeated a story a friend had told me of how her husband, after a long motorbike ride on a freezing cold night, had stripped off to stand naked in front of a roaring fire to get warmed ... Jay started to laugh and said, *Gives a new slant to Chestnuts Roasting on an Open Fire ...*

There was still a long way to go at that time before we reached the day when we had an argument over some trivial incident, both of us got cross, then agreed on a compromise – and I later realized that there had been no *You don't love me, you hate me, nobody loves me!*, which had been Anorexia's endless refrain. It had been years since a similar "good" argument with Jay. Funny how you can appreciate a row!

Discussions about all sorts of things – news items, interests and activities old and new – were another sign of Jay's return, having vanished completely when Anorexia came to live in our house. Apart from an all-consuming obsession with food and everything connected with it – including what everyone else was eating and had eaten during the day or days beforehand, recipes that had to be discussed and evaluated at length ingredient by ingredient, the offering of snacks at five-minute intervals – Anorexia had lost the ability to reason and to concentrate. With other cases of starvation (e.g., in wartime concentration camps or during famine), rational thought usually returns when a certain weight is reached, but even when she had reached a reasonable weight for her height it still took some considerable time for Jay's personality to slowly re-emerge and Anorexia to retreat. Very occasionally, when Jay is under stress and very tired, Anorexia appears briefly – but now it is possible for me to say just that, that I can hear Anorexia talking again. *Nobody loves me, nobody cares* ... And Jay is able to consider, talk about what is really bothering her, visit a friend for a chat, go to bed early and kick the unwelcome visitor out unceremoniously. I hope and pray that Anorexia will never make another long-term visit, but I know that when stress builds up there is always the possibility of a relapse. Jay will always have to fight off her attentions and be aware of that when life gets difficult.

One of the main signs of Jay's recovery is that she has gradually been able to again take more responsibility in sharing the cooking and shopping for the household. As Jay is a much better cook than I am, I am happy to let her cook again, knowing that amounts will be realistic. Shopping has returned to pre-anorexia patterns, with a "big" shop once a week topped up by occasional bits and pieces if we forget something or have unexpected visitors.

It is only when you lose someone that you really appreciate how much you loved and valued that person. Even all their annoying little habits are vastly preferable to the space left when they are not there. This is true when someone moves away whether through work, because of divorce, or for any other reason, especially true when a loved one dies. In each of these cases we recognize that a period of mourning takes place. But when a much loved person's personality undergoes a change beyond recognition, especially if that change also includes hostility and suspicion, the pain of loss, of bewilderment, of rejection is ongoing and may be there for many years. All the feelings of loss are often exacerbated by the lack of understanding by others.

The last few years have meant a very steep learning curve for me. Call it character building or what you will, I feel I have changed from the person I was at the beginning of Anorexia's invasion of my family, my house, my life as well as that of my daughter. While I would rather neither Jay nor myself had ever had experience of this devastating illness, at the same time I feel I have learned so much, not only about anorexia nervosa and other illnesses and the wide variety of individual responses to them, but also about what is really important in life. I've re-evaluated my whole life and what is important in it, what I want to do with the remaining years of it.

This book has been written for carers by a carer – my final message is **Keep going, don't give up! Don't give in to**

Anorexia or Bulimia. **If you do, your daughter, or your son, or your partner, is at grave risk. Look for help, look for what you need and keep going. The going may get rough, but you can do it. Keep going:**

> *I am working with a client with an eating disorder who says that she can't believe that after <u>sixteen years</u> of struggle she now feels that she is beginning to win the battle!*
>
> (Jane Knox, specialist dietician)

So, change is possible, even after many years of struggle.

Don't give up, keep going. Good luck on the long road.

Appendices

Definitions

Definitions are difficult ...

Given the complicated, interconnected, physical, psychological and emotional factors of anorexia nervosa, both the "straight" restrictive form and the binge–purge form, plus the individual differences present in eating disorders and the possible changes from anorexic phase to bulimic and back, it is small wonder that trying to develop definitions to suit all cases has proved so difficult over centuries. Therefore, the following may be taken as guidelines only, bearing in mind that each case may have one or more aspect that is outwith these definitions, sometimes referred to as an Eating Disorder Not Otherwise Specified (EDNOS).

Restrictive anorexia nervosa   The sufferer refuses any food and sometimes liquid. The sufferer is obsessed with body image, food and a desperate need to control and restrict intake. Compulsive exercise is frequently part of the illness.

Binge–purge anorexia nervosa   The sufferer does not wish to eat, but starving leads to his or her body crying out for sustenance, and when the sufferer gives in she binges, then purges what has been eaten by vomiting or using laxatives. A cycle of bingeing and starving becomes established, with bingeing being experienced along with strong self-disgust at the lack of control followed by renewed attempts at starvation. The sufferer is obsessed with body image, food and a desperate need to control and restrict intake. Compulsive exercise is frequently part of the picture. In both types of anorexia nervosa, such distorted thinking means that, even at a life-threateningly low weight, Anorexia will claim to be fat, resulting in relationships being affected as behaviour changes.

Bulimia nervosa   The sufferer is obsessed with body image, food and a desperate need to control and restrict intake through purging by vomiting or using laxatives. Sometimes this is used as a way to control weight and the sufferer may be of light weight but within normal guidelines.

Carer   *A person who supports or looks after family, partners or friends in need of help because they are ill, frail or have a disability. The care they provide is unpaid* (Scottish Mental Health and Well Being Support Group). *A person who has had to change their life-style in order to care for and/or take responsibility for another individual who is experiencing mental health problems* (Clinical Standards Board for Scotland – Schizophrenia). *The strain on these informal carers can be severe, resulting in an increased risk of both physical and mental ill health. It is important to review how the carer is managing and to encourage them to find ways of reducing the stress on them* (WHO, 2001).

Some facts . . .

- **Both types of anorexia nervosa can be life-threatening** because of the effects of starvation. As in other obsessions, compulsions and addictions, sufferers frequently and vehemently deny they have a problem.
- **Bulimia nervosa can also be life-threatening** due to mineral imbalances (e.g., lack of potassium may result in a heart attack).
- **About 10% of sufferers are male.**
- The majority of sufferers are between 15 and 25 when the problems begin, but the illnesses may begin at any age. The

illnesses may develop or continue at a much older age, and there are unfortunately now children as young as 6 who develop anorexia and/or bulimia.

- Eating disorders are among the most common disorders of adolescence.
- The behaviour causes huge problems, not only for sufferers but also great stress and much frustration for families, many of whom feel overwhelmed.
- Despite centuries of medical debate and many theories and treatments, no single cause has been found.
- Success in the treatment of anorexia nervosa varies, with about 80% making a recovery. (The quality of recovery may vary.)
- Given the frequent reluctance of sufferers to acknowledge problems and their ambivalence about treatment involving changes in lifestyle and eating habits, statistics for bulimia (without anorexia) can only be estimated.
- Research currently continues into genetic links that cause vulnerability under stressful conditions.

Family areas affected by anorexia and bulimia nervosa

Mealtimes   To comment or not when portions are unusually big or small, when there are bizarre food combinations, etc.

Cooking   Ingredients may be missing following a binge.

Shopping   A "weekly" shop may disappear overnight.

Time   More frequent shopping takes up more time (and energy).

Finance   Extra food, cleaning items, plumbing, heating costs.

Plumbing   Undigested food can affect drains, especially in old houses.

Heating   Low body temperatures mean extra heating.

Social life   Difficult to invite friends in when there might not be any biscuits, sugar, food for breakfast, etc. Difficult to entertain if you aren't sure about ingredients being there when you go to cook. Difficult to go out when to do so is seen as rejection. Friends and family find it difficult to know how to react to unusual behaviour, especially aggression.

All relationships   Different views about how to react to anorexia and bulimia nervosa can cause many problems in the immediate family (e.g., when no food is left, when money has been taken to fund a binge, feelings of lack of attention for other family members).

Work relationships, friendships Whether to discuss the problem or not?

Sleep Loss of sleep through worry about the sufferer's health, family disintegration, other siblings/partner being neglected. Night binges may waken family. Sufferer may wake family angrily because of some incident that has happened in his or her life, often unrelated to the family. Difficult to get off to sleep for anticipation of further similar incidents.

Work Lack of sleep, concentration difficulties and other effects of long-term stress will affect work.

Trust If sufferer has lied about activities (e.g., has stolen money or been shoplifting), it's difficult to regain trust once it has been broken. After being told lies, you want to trust and believe, but it's hard to accept you're being told the truth.

More carers' conversations from the EDA helpline and meetings

Without being a fly on the wall it is hard for sympathetic friends, or even experienced professionals who only see Anorexia or Bulimia in the structured environment of a clinic or hospital, to imagine how very different behaviour can be in different situations. Often appearing extremely compliant at times, Anorexia and Bulimia can change to the opposite at home. At different stages, possibly depending on stress levels in life outside the home, Anorexia may appear with a vengeance for an hour or two, a day or two, a week or two, even months, only to vanish for a while then reappear unpredictably later. During rational times sufferers may be able to recognize the extremes of behaviour – one sufferer observed: *When the illness is very strong, I'm not myself. I'm someone else.* Fighting to make Anorexia relax that ferocious grip needs huge amounts of willpower and determination in the battle to regain control. Watching that battle, feeling a helpless bystander, is a living nightmare for families who want to help; yet unless their loved one recognizes the problem and actively wants to get better, they can do little apart from their utmost to motivate toward change. Efforts at motivation take long-term energy, stamina and teamwork as well as patience.

Some of these stories are harrowing and grim. As one professional pointed out to me, often listeners on a helpline hear only the
worst cases – if treatment is prompt and effective, then there is
little reason to phone a helpline at all. If you are reading this as a
carer at the beginning of the road, perhaps after recent diagnosis, it
is important to remember that diagnosis may not mean the same
for your loved one as for anyone else. But being prepared by
finding out what is possible when Anorexia and/or Bulimia move
in, as well as considering possible strategies for various situations
and eventualities, is probably the best defence in what may be a
long battle.

Each case is individual. In many cases the very worst behaviour some carers speak about is absent. Only through listening on
the helpline have I learned that my own experience with Jay is
different from that of many others. The decisions I faced were
extremely difficult; only with hindsight can I now say this or
that really helped or was a mistake, but listening on the helpline
has made me very thankful that I have not had personal experience
of some of these dilemmas ...

■ *I keep thinking that the worst has happened, it can't get any*
worse. And then it does. My daughter is now 28. She was
diagnosed with AN when she was 15 and was an inpatient
for several months. When she came home she seemed better
for quite a while and went to college, started work ... and
then she met someone she wanted to marry. It was after the
relationship ended that she lost weight again, only this time she
started bingeing as well as over-exercising and abusing laxa-
tives. She borrowed a lot of money from us, we know now she
spent it on food, which she got rid of in one way or another. She
lost her job, then she started stealing money from friends.
Shoplifting too. We've paid fines for her ... it's the first time
anyone in our family has been in trouble with the police. In this
small community, everyone knows and my mother has stopped
going out at all, she's so terribly upset. I find it difficult to
work, knowing that everyone who comes into the shop knows.
One part of me says it's a terrible illness, we've done nothing
wrong, but the other part just wants to crawl away and die.
Now she's in trouble again, owes thousands of pounds on store

cards this time. I think she sold the things to get food. Should we pay off her debts or let her go to court again?

■ *We tried locking the bathroom door to stop her getting rid of food. So she used towels in her room. Her room is an absolute tip, but if I say anything she says if I don't like it I can clean it up. I think she should clear up her own mess, but she never does and the house smells. What should I do?*

■ *My son was in hospital for months, with AN. When he came home he got a job. Things are OK during the week when he is working, but he has started going out with his pals at weekends, not eating anything over the weekend. Now he's drinking heavily every weekend, sometimes doesn't come home. Twice he hasn't been able to go to work on Mondays because he's been so hungover. I think he'll lose his job if he can't control his drinking, but if I try to talk to him he just says everyone drinks and stop nagging him. I can't bear watching him ruining his life. My other son has moved out because he can't cope with his brother's behaviour, and I hardly see him now.*

■ (Over four years and many phone calls) *We were able to send my daughter to good schools, we tried to give her all the things we never had. Both my wife and I came up the hard way, and we just wanted to give her the opportunities we didn't have when we were children. Then she went to college; that's when it all went wrong, but we didn't know for a long time. We bought her a flat and furnished it for her, a car and everything to help her. I suppose we spoiled her, we had the money and it seemed mean not to give her the best when we could. She kept asking for a bigger allowance and we gave it. Then more and more, it was never enough. We know now that it went on food. ... When she finally agreed to see a doctor her eating was out of control, she'd given up college and all her friends. She was bingeing and getting rid of it lots and lots of times in a day, it was just horrible to know what she was doing. If we said anything there was another row, it didn't matter what we said. We paid for private treatment, but it didn't really make much difference, she just went back to her old ways when she came out. It never took long. ... The flat was in her name and she sold it to get money. Spent it all. The doctor said to stop giving her more than enough for one day, so then she got into trouble for stealing food and drink. We were told to try to make her face up to being responsible for her behaviour and she was charged and appeared in court. She didn't want to come home, said she couldn't stand us trying to change her. She ended up eventually with the Cyrenians, who were the only people who would take her in. ... I thought it might help if I was at home all the time, so I took early retirement. I had a good job, but everything has gone on paying for her treatment, there's not much left now. My wife and I have split up, I think because of all the strain. ... My daughter is back with the Cyrenians. I just don't know how it will all end, I am so afraid for her. But she has promised not to drink again so maybe that's hopeful, maybe this time they'll be able to help her. ... She has lost her place in the Cyrenian hostel, their rule is no drinking on the premises and she started drinking again. I just can't bear the thought of her actually in the gutter, so I let her sleep here. I cook for her if she wants food, but don't give her any money. So she just goes out and steals so she can binge or drink. I've lost all my friends, I don't really see anyone now, it's too difficult to try to explain when they ask about my family. ... One of the doctors said maybe I just have to let her reach the gutter and then maybe she might recognize she's the only person who can change things. I can't bear the thought of my daughter, my only child, in the gutter, I can't put her out.*

I know I shouldn't give in to all his demands, but I get so tired of it all. My son has been ill for five years with bulimia, but I don't think many people would ever guess. Everyone thinks he's such a lovely man, but he's like a different person when he comes home. His temper is awful, but he looks just a normal weight, not particularly thin or anything. The worst was when I heard a noise during the night and came down and found him in the middle of a binge. He'd even eaten what was in the freezer, frozen. Often now I lie awake, but I stay in my room. He needs help, but he won't listen to me, I don't know what to do. Should I tell him to get a place of his own, somehow make him leave? He'd hate me for it.

■ *Our family is cracking up because of my daughter's illness. She's 23 now and really horrible to her younger sisters. They're 14 and 17. I think she feels they've got everything she hasn't, although she was good at school and better than either of them at art. She's really talented in art and wanted to be an illustrator, even started a course, but gave it up. She's been in hospital twice for treatment for her eating disorder, but both times when she came out she regressed quite quickly; this is the third time. This time I'm thinking of saying she can't come home again here when she's discharged, I feel I have to protect the other two. But I don't know what'll happen to her, where else she could go. And if she's ill, surely I shouldn't be thinking of abandoning her ... but I've got to think of my other daughters too. What's the best thing to do?*

■ *My friends think my daughter is really charming, she's so pleasant when anyone else is here. The GP thinks the same, he's a friend of ours. How can I possibly tell them what life is really like at home?*

■ *I've taken my daughter to our GP several times. She's lost a lot of weight over about three months, maybe as much as three stones, and is all skin and bone. Two weeks ago he said she can lose another 10 pounds before we need to worry. He thinks I'm just a fussing parent and I really don't want to go back again but my daughter is still losing weight. How long do you think I should wait? Do you think I should go to another GP?*

■ *My daughter is absolutely phobic about food, it's as if she thinks it will poison her. Last week my son dropped a whole bottle of tomato sauce on the kitchen floor and my daughter started screaming because she was so afraid it might have splashed her when it smashed. She doesn't want to go to school because people have biscuits and crisps in their bags for break, and she doesn't want to stay for school dinners any more. She's stopped eating properly and even threatened to stop drinking at one point last month. We were told waiting lists to see a specialist are at least 10 months and we can't afford to go private. Should we make her go to school while we wait for an appointment? So far we've made her go, but it's a daily battle and we're all exhausted. Or should we let her stay at home as she wants?*

▨ *It's like living with a volcano in the house, waiting for the next explosion. Everybody sort of tiptoes around her, afraid to upset her. She knows that and uses it to get what she wants.*

▨ *My husband is on the verge of leaving – he says he can't take any more. He thinks I'm much too soft with her. I don't know what to do.*

▨ *My daughter is 19, was in hospital for months and came home much better, but she can't find a job and has nothing to do during the day. She's tried really hard to find work, even voluntary work, but there's nothing in this area. Now she's getting really depressed and her eating is not nearly as good – she's started eating alone again, won't join in things and gets angry over the least little thing. I'm afraid it's starting all over again and I don't know what to do. I feel depressed myself at the thought of going through it all again.*

▨ *My doctor says I should "make her stand on her own two feet, make her be independent". If I told her to move out and get her own place, she'd see it as rejection. Anyway, how can you put someone emotionally about 10 out to fend for themselves?*

▨ (Over several calls and meetings) *My daughter has had eating problems for six years ... Our GP has done all sorts of tests and can find no explanation for the stomach pains she complains of ... She's seen a dietician, a psychiatrist but both said there was nothing wrong with her. Six weeks ago my daughter almost stopped eating and another appointment was made with a psychiatrist, who told her she "just had to eat", and told me I "just had to make my daughter eat". When we came out, my daughter said that if I went on about her not eating any more, she would stop drinking as well. My daughter has been admitted to hospital for observation as her BMI [Body Mass Index] is so low. Now the psychiatrist says my daughter is just malnour-*

ished and it's my fault because of my anxiety. I've been told to stop attending support meetings because it could make my daughter anxious. The psychiatrist says she doesn't have anorexia but it's maybe another eating disorder. Everything I've read or heard fits in with AN [Anorexia Nervosa] *and I'm so worried.*

▪ *My son was in a private hospital for several months. He's home now and got a job. At first everything was really good but now I'm afraid he's going to relapse. Things are fine as long as he's working, but everything goes haywire at the weekends and he binges repeatedly and all the rows are starting again. He stays in the bathroom for hours and no one else can get in. He has to share a room with his little brother who wants to leave home; he says he can't stand living here any more. We love both our children and did lots of things together before my son got anorexia and bulimia, but this is tearing us apart. I thought we were a happy family until four years ago. Now ...*

▪ (Over nine months, calls and meetings) *My daughter is 14 and was "sectioned" as she wouldn't agree to go into hospital – the doctor said she would die without hospital treatment, her BMI was so low. She was taken to an adolescent unit miles and miles away from home. We often went to visit her, my husband took time off work so that he could come too and other members of the family went too on their own, but she often said she didn't want to see any of us and we just had to leave again. She hates us because she says we sent her away, but she would have died otherwise. She says the most awful things ... In hospital she told staff that she would do what she was told and then they would have no reason to keep her in – she stopped all her rituals and ate her meals until she had reached the required weight, then demanded to be released. She even argued with the mental health authorities and won her case – she's only 14! The authorities wrote to her that she was no longer under section and she discharged herself. Staff said that they couldn't stop her leaving when she walked out ... She came home and stopped eating, started all her rituals again, also physically attacked her younger brothers; they're afraid of her and they're very badly affected by the whole situation. She's horrible to me and my husband and sometimes I find myself retaliating. What should I do when she's violent? ... Eventually she agreed to return voluntarily to the unit. Part of being admitted to the unit involves education in their classroom, now she's refused to attend the class. If she won't comply with the rules, the unit say she can't be there. What are we going to do? If she comes home I think she'll destroy our family, the boys are terrified, yet I can't abandon her – she's my child but I can't recognize the girl we brought up ... What's going to happen to her, what's going to happen to us? The unit has been closed. Now we have the choice of bringing our daughter – now 15 – home (she's violent to her younger brothers as well as to us), or putting her into care. Her hatred and aggression are so awful – our family is disintegrating.*

With stories such as these, facing enemies like Anorexia and Bulimia who employ every possible devious trick to gain control yet can at the same time seem quite reasonable to outsiders, who can doubt that families as well as sufferers need help and support as early as possible to prevent these illnesses becoming entrenched and chronic, and often life-threatening?

For years I seemed to live in a different world from my family. I just didn't believe them when they said they loved me. When they tried to help, I thought they were against me. Nothing made any sense. The pain inside was awful, but I couldn't let anyone help for a long time. The people closest to me were the ones I behaved worst with, maybe because inside I trusted them not to leave me no matter what I did. I feel very bad now about the hell I put my mother through.

(A former sufferer)

Eating disorders can and do destroy not only sufferers' lives – at their worst blighting hopes of independent adult life with all its glorious ups and downs and wasting so many talents along the way – but also the lives of whole families. Yet until recently eating disorders were quite often dismissed as trivial!

Addiction/compulsive behaviour – going down ... coming up!

There are recognizable stages in developing an addiction or compulsive behaviour, and there are corresponding recognizable stages for the parent/partner/main carer of an addict. There are many similarities between the experiences of families coping with addictions and alcoholism, and those coping with anorexia and bulimia. Here is an outline of behaviours with possible/probable behaviour of carers and family given below in italics. For *"addict"* read *"anorexia/bulimia"*; for *"substance"* read *"food abuse"* – self-starvation or binge/vomit cycle; for *"codependent"* read *"carer"* (based on Arthur Wassmer, 1990).

Going down ...

The addict is reacting to changes produced by his or her use of his or her substance – drugs, alcohol, etc.
The codependent reacts to changes in his or her addict.

First regular use of substance.
Attraction to potential addict who seems an exciting, romantic, "glittering" person, always "on the go", active and doing.

Social life begins to change to include substance use.
"Goes along" with social changes, tries to fit in.

Growing preoccupation with substance.
Accepts substance as part of normal life. May obtain substance for addict.

Increase in tolerance to substance.
Accepts, ignores, even defends increased use. Quells his or her own fears.

Onset of memory blackouts.
Frustration with addict's lapses. Sometimes wonders if it is she or he (i.e., the carer) who is crazy.

Guilt about substance abuse/surreptitious use of substance.
Feels appeased by addict's guilt about substance use. Accepts his or her promises, expressions of remorse.

Refusal to talk about substance use or problems caused by growing dependence on it.
Accepts refusal to acknowledge or talk about substance use. Is intimidated by addict's defensive anger. Begins to "act out" anger.

Loss of control, inability to stop when others do or when intends to.
Thoughts, attitudes, decisions governed by addict's behaviour. Life becomes coping with a series of emergencies.

Rationalizations and excuses.
Rationalizations and excuses for addict's behaviour. "Someone's got to take care of things, hold things together." Build up of anger and loss of respect for addict.

Grandiose, aggressive behaviour.
Disgusted by grandiosity, terrified by aggression, becomes increasingly withdrawn, silently enraged.

Attempts to control use fail.
*Attempts to control addict's use by looking for hidden supplies, manip-
ulating activity, extracting promises, lecturing, haranguing.*

Use becomes constant. Family and friends avoided. Work, money
worries pile up.
*Accepts social isolation – not worth the embarrassment. Assumes more
responsibility for breadwinning and financial management.*

Irrational thinking, build up of resentments. May steal to fund the
habit.
*Drawn into endless irrational arguments and discussions. Takes
addict's resentment personally.*

Complete inability to function socially, sexually, occupationally.
Accepts social withdrawal. Completely takes over breadwinner role.

Physical symptoms of dependence may include shakes, uncon-
sciousness, liver disease, withdrawal symptoms, psychological
symptoms resembling mental illness.
*Develops stress-related physical problems. May seem crazy to friends.
Traumatic medical emergencies may occur.*

"Hits bottom". Using substance and living becomes an either/or
choice. Next step – **either death or recovery**.
*Hits bottom as well. May leave addict, commit suicide or think ser-
iously about it.* ***Or begin to recover.***

Coming up!

Breakthrough of denial – admits defeat, addiction and its effects.
Chronic depression. Locked into misery. Gives up on addict or self.

Accepts the need for treatment, enters treatment. Implosion of
personality. Withdrawal. Depression.
*At end of tether, actively seeks help (through Al Anon or other
organizations).*

Learns addiction/compulsive behaviour is a disease. First hope.
Learns about "codependency". First hope.

Withdrawal symptoms subside. Feels better. Appearance gets better.
Emotional storm subsides. Feels more in control.

Psychologically improves. Thinking is clearer, mood improves.
Starts to think more appropriately/rationally about situation.

Leaves treatment. Fears about new life. If alcoholic, starts AA. Looks for support.
Begins healthy focus on self rather than addict.

Fears diminish. Begins to appreciate life without substance.
Anxiety and depression diminish. Stops enabling and takes responsibility.

New friends, new work, new activities.
New friends, new activities.

Appreciates advantages of life without substance. Feels physically much better.
Experiences/enjoys benefits of developing healthy behaviours.

Must deal with "wreckage of the past".
Must deal with "wreckage of the past".

High danger of relapse.
Counselling begins to focus on emotional and spiritual issues.

Begins to deal with emotional and spiritual issues. Gets counselling.
Healthy self-interest. Feels stable and sane.

Understands self. Eliminates self-defeating, self-harming behaviour. Spiritual growth.
Happiness is based on inner rather than outer factors. Spiritual growth.

In recovery, addict reaches greater-than-average degree of emotional and spiritual understanding.
Reaches greater-than-average degree of emotional and spiritual understanding.

When I found this outline of recognized stages for addiction/compulsive behaviour, and frequently the corresponding stages for the families of those affected, I was stunned by the parallels between experiences. And I wept, because I could see clearly that far from helping, Anxious Annie and Soft Sue in their anxiety and worry were not helping Anorexia or Bulimia, but actually supporting the behaviour. Not every family or carer, not every sufferer, will follow the same path exactly in the same order, but the sequence, the downward spiral in tandem, is a frequent pattern. It is only on recognition of the depths of the problems and their effects on individual lives, followed by positive sustained action to address these, that recovery is possible.

How to be a motivational carer

From a workshop led by Gill Todd at the EDA Carers' Conference 2000

No one will change because they have been told to. People change only when they themselves recognize a need for change.

One of the features of anorexia nervosa is a fear of change. The aim of the workshop is to explore and resolve ambivalence. Remember the story of the sun and the wind's battle to get a man to take off his coat? The wind blew and raged and battled with the man, but not only did he keep on his coat, he did up all the buttons, turned up the collar and held on tight to it. The sun smiled and shone gently and warmly ... and the man recognized that he needed to change. The stages for change are:

- Precontemplation – not really ready to change.
- Contemplation – thinking toward change.
- Preparation – gathering oneself.
- Action – making the change.
- Maintenance – following through ...
- Relapse – didn't make it this time. Try again ...

Perhaps you can identify at which stage your daughter, son, partner is at just now by his or her behaviour.

Carers should try to:

- be as warm and caring as possible;
- let her explain her arguments for change or for staying the same;
- focus on her concerns;
- stress **choice** and responsibility;
- discuss the pros and cons of different choices;
- repeat and reflect what you feel she means;
- summarize periodically;
- admit when you make mistakes;
- avoid saying BUT ...
- be prepared to talk about own role.

Carers should try to avoid:

- lecturing, arguing;
- assuming an authoritarian role;
- assuming expert role;
- ordering, directing, threatening;
- doing most of the talking;
- getting into debates about labels;
- making moral statements;
- criticizing, preaching, or judging;
- asking three questions in a row;
- outlining what YOU think is the problem;
- prescribing solutions;
- attempts to persuade with logic.

The carer's job is to support in the process of change, to encourage and give confidence that change is possible, that she can cope with change.

Try to find times to talk when the atmosphere is relaxed, perhaps when just sitting around on a Sunday morning, or when out for a walk, rather than try to "set up" a discussion. Be prepared to listen to, rather than talk at.

Be prepared for a long road with two steps forward and one back. As on all long journeys, look out for support, look after yourself, give yourself breaks – a carer is there when no one else is left.

Useful addresses, phone numbers and websites

Eating Disorder Association

103 Prince of Wales Road
Norwich NR1 1DW
United Kingdom
Email **info@edauk.com**
Telephone helpline – **0845 634 1414** (Monday–Friday,
    8.30 a.m.–8.30 p.m.)
Youth helpline – **0845 634 7650** (Monday–Friday, 4–6.30 p.m.)

The EDA will give contact numbers for local self-help groups and
contacts where possible.

Internet

Two of the best sites are:

- **www.edauk.com**
- **www.eatingresearch.com**

There are thousands of Internet sites referring to eating disorders.
Some are very helpful and give very interesting and accurate

information, others are rubbish. If you have little or no experience it is difficult to know what is useful or useless.

Local Health Services

May be able to offer local contacts – try your GP, your local library or Social Work departments for addresses.

Samaritans

Tel. **0845 790 9090** (24-hour service).

Recommended reading

Eating Disorder Association Carers' Guide (2002, EDA, Norwich, UK) – practical, informative and supportive in a simple, clear, concise and well-laid-out form. Everything you need!

Anorexia nervosa: a survival guide for families, friends and sufferers (Janet Treasure, 1997, Psychology Press, Hove, UK) – written specifically for carers, this book gives invaluable support and help as well as such interesting and relevant information as the psychological effects of starvation, an outline of medical theories, assumptions and treatments throughout the ages.

My Body, My Enemy (Claire Beeken, 1997, Thorsons, London) and *Hungry Hell* (Kate Chisholm, 2002, Short Books, London) – give insight into the thinking behind anorexia nervosa – or "Anorexia" – that may help carers to accept their family members' difficulties, feelings and behaviour while supporting them in their struggle with the illness.

Recovering Together: How to Help an Alcoholic without Hurting Yourself (Arthur Wassmer, 1990, Henry Holt, New York) – although intended for the families of alcoholics and addicts it may also be helpful for carers of Anorexia and Bulimia.

Anorexia Nervosa and Bulimia: How to Help (Marilyn Duker and Roger Slade, 1997, Open University Press, Buckingham, UK) – written for professionals, but interesting and useful reading.

The Anorexic Experience (Marilyn Lawrence, 1995, The Women's Press, London).

Any publication recommended by the EDA is worth reading. In my search for information and help, I have found useful items in many places – libraries, bookstalls, bookshops, Internet sites – and have asked friends to be on the lookout for interesting reading.

Bibliography

Andersen, A. (1985) *Practical Comprehensive Treatment of Anorexia Nervosa and Bulimia*, Johns Hopkins University Press, Baltimore.

Asen, E. (1995) *Family Therapy for Everyone – How to Get the Best out of Living Together*, BBC Books, London.

Beattie, M. (1987) *Codependent No More: How to Stop Controlling Others and Start Caring for Yourself*, Hazelden, MN.

Beeken, C. (1997) *My Body, My Enemy*, Thorsons, London.

Bolton, R. (1986) *People Skills* (A Touchstone Book), Simon and Schuster, New York.

Bruch, H. (1973) *Eating Disorders: Obesity, Anorexia Nervosa and the Person Within*, Basic Books, New York.

Bruch, H. (1982) *Anorexia Nervosa: Therapy and Theory*, American Psychiatric Association, New York.

Buckroyd, J. (1996) *Anorexia and Bulimia – The Element Guide*, Element Books, London.

Callaghan, M. (1989) *Wrinkles on the Heart*, Alabaster Press, Grove City, OH.

Carter, R. (1994) *Helping Yourself to Help Others – A Book for Caregivers*, Times Books, New York.

Chisholm, K. (2002) *Hungry Hell*, Short Books, London.

Connan, F. and Treasure, J. (2000) Working with adults with anorexia nervosa in an out-patient setting, *Advances in Psychiatric Treatment*, **6**, 135–144.

Crisp, A., Joughmin, N., Halek, C. and Bowyer, C. (1996) *Anorexia Nervosa: The Wish to Change*, Psychology Press, Hove, UK.

Dare, C., Eisler, I., Russell, G., Treasure, J. and Dodge, L. (2001) Psychological therapies for adults with anorexia nervosa: Randomised controlled trial of outpatient treatments, *British Journal of Psychiatry*, **178**, 216–221.

Dawsen, D. (2001) *Anorexia and Bulimia: A Parent's Guide to Recognising Eating Disorders and Taking Control*, Vermilion, London.

DoH (2001) *The Expert Patient: A New Approach to Chronic Disease Management for the Twenty-first Century*, Department of Health, London (**www.ohn.gov.uk/people/expert.htm**).

Duker, M. and Slade, R. (1997) *Anorexia Nervosa and Bulimia: How to Help*, Open University Press, Buckingham, UK.

EDA Carers' Guide (2002), Eating Disorders Association, Norwich, UK.

Fennell, M. (1999) *Overcoming Low Self-esteem: A Self-help Guide Using Cognitive Behavioural Techniques*, Robinson Publishing, London.

Forward, S. (1989) *Toxic Parents: Overcoming Their Legacy and Reclaiming Your Life*, Bantam, London.

Goleman, D. (1993) *Emotional Intelligence*, Bloomsbury Publishing, London.

Haigh, R. and Treasure, J. (2002) Investigating the needs of carers in the area of eating disorders: Development of the carers' Needs Assessment Measure (CaNAM), *European Eating Disorders Review*, **10**, 1–17.

Herbert, C. and Wetmore, A. (1999) *Overcoming Traumatic Stress – A Self-help Guide Using Cognitive Behavioural Techniques*, Robinson Publishing, London.

HH Dalai Lama and Cutler, H. (1999) *The Art of Happiness: A Handbook for Living*, Hodder & Stoughton, London.

Jaffa, T., Honig, P., Farmer, S. and Dilley, J. (2002) Family meals in the treatment of adolescent anorexia nervosa, *European Eating Disorders Review*, **10**, 199–207.

Janet, P. (1903) *The Major Symptoms of Hysteria*, Macmillan, London.

Lambley, P. (1983) *How to Surivve Anorexia*, Frederick Muller, London.

Lawrence, M. (1995) *The Anorexic Experience*, The Women's Press, London.

Leff, J. (1994) Working with the families of schizophrenic patients, *British Journal of Psychiatry*, **164**(suppl. 23), 71–76.

Lorig, K. (n.d.) *Chronic Disease Self-Management Program (CDSMP)* (A research programme), The Patient Education Research Center, Stanford University, Palo Alto, CA.

Lovell, D. (2000) *Lives in the Balance*, Eagle Publishing, Guildford, UK.

McCormack, E. (2000) Paper given at *Stress Management Workshop, Aberdeen, November 2000*.

McCormick, E. W. (1990) *Change for the Better*, Cassell, London.

McWilliams, J.-R. and McWilliams, P. (1991) *You Can't Afford the Luxury of a Negative Thought* (A book for people with life-threatening illness – including life!), Thorsons, London (first published in 1986 by Prelude Press, Los Angeles).

Mearns, D., and Thorne, B. (1999) *Person-centred Counselling in Action*, Sage Publications, London.

Meyers, R. and Smith, J. (1995) *Clinical Guide to Alcohol Treatment: The Community Re-inforcement Approach*, Guilford Press, New York.

Mueser, K. and Gingerich, S. (1994) *Coping with Schizophrenia – A Guide for Families*, New Harbinger Publications, Oakland, CA.

Nielsen, S., Moller-Madsen, S., Isager, T., Jorgensen, J., Pagsberg, K. and Theander, S. (1998) Standardised mortality in eating disorders – A quantitative summary of previously published and new evidence, *Journal of Psychosomatic Research*, **44**, 413–434.

Page, L., Sutherby, K. and Treasure, J. (2002) A preliminary description of the use of relapse management cards in anorexia nervosa, *European Eating Disorders Review*, **10**(4).

Peck, M. S. (1990) *The Road Less Travelled*, Arrow Books, London (first published in 1983 by Hutchinson, UK).

Prochaska, J. O. and Di Climente, C. C. (1992) *The Transtheoretical Model for Change: Handbook of Psychotherapy Integration*, Basic Books, New York.

Quilliam, S. (1998) *The Samaritans Book of What to Do When You Really Want to Help But Don't Know How*, Transformation Press, Essex, UK.

Ramsay, R., Gerada, G., Mars, S. and Szmukler, G. (eds) (2001) *Mental Illness: A Handbook for Carers*, Jessica Kingsley, London.

Reas, D. L., Williamson, D. A., Martin, C. K. and Zucker, N. L. (2000) Duration of illness predicts outcome for bulimia nervosa: A long-term follow-up study, *International Journal of Eating Disorders*, **27**, 428–434.

Ryle, J. (1936) Anorexia nervosa, *Lancet*, **ii**, 893–899.

Sams, C. (2003) *The Little Food Book*, Alistair Sawday Publishing, Bristol.

Schmidt, U. (2003) Mandometer musings, *European Eating Disorders Review*, **11**(1).

Schmidt, U. and Treasure, J. L. (1993) *Getting Better Bite(e) by Bit(e)*, Psychology Press, Hove, UK.

Schmidt, U., Bone, G., Hems, S., Lennem, J. and Treasure, J. (2002) Structured therapeutic writing tasks as an adjunct to treatment in eating disorders, *European Eating Disorders Review*, **10**(5).

Scholz, M. and Asen, E. (2001) Multiple family therapy with eating disordered adolescents: Concepts and preliminary results, *European Eating Disorders Review*, **9**.

Sczmuker, G., Dare, C. and Treasure, J. (1995) *Handbook of Eating Disorders: Theory, Treatment and Research*, John Wiley and Sons, Chichester, UK.

Skynner, R. and Cleese, J. (1989) *Families and How to Survive Them*, Mandarin, London.

Tannen, D. (1992) *You Just Don't Understand*, Virago, London.

Treasure, J. (1997) *Anorexia nervosa: a survival guide for families, friends and sufferers*, Psychology Press, Hove, UK.

Treasure, J. and Schmidt, U. (2001) Ready, willing and able to change: Motivational aspects of the assessment and treatment of eating disorders, *European Eating Disorders Review*, **9**, 4–18.

Treasure, J., Murphy, T., Szmukler, G., Todd, G., Gavan, K. and Joyce, J. (2001) The experience of caregiving for severe mental illness: A comparison between anorexia nervosa and psychosis, *Society Psychiatry Psychiatric Epidemiology*, **36**, 343–347.

Treasure, J., Gavan, K., Todd, G. and Schmidt, U. (2003) Changing the environment in eating disorders: Working with carers and families to improve motivation and facilitate change, *European Eating Disorders Review*, **11**(1).

Treasure, J., Schmidt, U. and van Furth, E. (2003) *Handbook of Eating Disorders: Theory, Treatment and Research* (2nd edn), John Wiley & Sons, Chichester, UK.

Tse, M. (1995) *Qigong for Health and Vitality*, Piatkus Books, London.

Velicer, W. F., Prochaska, J. O., Rossi, J. and Di Clemente, C. C. (1996) A criterion measurement model for addictive behaviors. *Addictive Behaviors*, **21**, 555–584.

Waskett, C. (1993) *Counselling People in Eating Distress*, British Association for Counselling, Rugby, UK.

Wassmer, A. (1993) *Recovering Together – How to Help an Alcoholic without Hurting Yourself*, Henry Holt, New York.

Whitaker, S. (1994) *The Good Retreat Guide*, Random House, London.

WHO (2000) *World Health Organisation Guide to Mental Health in Primary Care*, Royal Society of Medicine Press, London.

Yellowlees, A. (1997) *Working with Eating Disorders and Self-Esteem*, Folens, Dunstable, UK.

Index